INSIDE THE CLUB

Inside the Club.
Stories of the Employees of the Former Lake Placid Club.

You can contact the author at campbellba@earthlink.net

Book design and typography by Melissa Mykal Batalin.

Printed in the United States.
The Troy Book Makers.
Troy, New York.
www.thetroybookmakers.com

Cover postcard written by Marie Webster, 1930.

ISBN-13: 978-1-933994-74-1

INSIDE THE CLUB

Stories of the
employees of the former
Lake Placid Club

BARBARA A. CAMPBELL

CONTENTS

FOREWORD

Why am I interested in Lake Placid and the Lake Placid Club?

Well, blame it on my father!

He enjoyed going up to Lake Placid, N.Y., from Connecticut. He would bring his racing skates and I my figure skates to use on Mirror Lake. My parents, Gordon K. and Marguerite C. Campbell, and I would go to square dancing shows on ice and hockey games at the old Olympic Arena. We loved the challenge of the cold and the beauty of the mountains.

We knew that once the ice started to melt on the bobsled run at Mt. van Hoevenberg, the run would be closed to racing but open to kids. One year we brought my sled up to the bobsled run. Checking to see no one was coming around the curves Shady, Zigging or Zagging; Father helped me climb into the run. On Feb. 26, 1952 (I woodburned the date on the bottom of my sled), I got on my sled, rounded only the last curve to the finish line dragging the toes of my boots on the ice all the way!

Father talked about Lake Placid with his friends at the bank where he worked in Hartford, Conn. Al Dewey, Club member not related to Melville Dewey as far as we knew, suggested as long as we liked Lake Placid so much, why didn't we stay at the Club? We had dinner there, thought it was very nice and Mr. Dewey arranged for us to be Introduced Guests. We filled out no application, had the use of the Club and learned afterward we were classified as "Potential Members", "Possible Members" or "Do not encourage". I don't know how we ranked!

We would arrive at the Club with several inches of ice on our headlights after coming up as much of the Northway as was completed. On our way to breakfast, my father and I had to check the special thermometer that gave a pen and ink recording of how cold it had been the previous night, 24 degrees below not being unusual. Once in a while Father would put our car in the heated garage so we would be sure it would start in the morning.

We only visited during February school vacations. It was a long time before I knew Lake Placid had sidewalks. There was always so much snow and such high snowbanks! The Club menus reflected the February Presidents' holiday. I remember "Washington pie, and Betsy Ross salad."

I'm a reader and I enjoyed curling up with a book in front of the fireplace by the entrance. We all had fun at bingo on the balcony. The sound of the Colgate 13 singing downstairs was welcoming (especially since my grandmother, who was from Sherburne, N.Y., had dated the boys from Colgate College in the 1890s). I was glad to find a place where I could wear floor-length wool skirts to dinner. I remember one pale yellow plaid skirt and matching angora sweater that I knit in the early 1960s.

In 1968 I brought my pastels to the Club and drew a collection of daffodils forced in the greenhouse to blossom in the winter. The pastels now grace the walls of my house in Connecticut.

I used my skates frequently on the rink frozen on the tennis courts and skated Mother around on one of the chairs with runners.

Always one to think I could do anything, Father insisted I take downhill ski lessons at Mt. Whitney. He had skied on the campus of Trinity College in Hartford and I had played a little with his skis on the firemen's hill in back of our house. I joined the group on the bunny slope, learned the snowplow, and all of a sudden it was time to ride the ski lift. My memory is that I was shivering and standing sideways on the mountain, the downhill ski 12 inches lower than its mate! The lodge looked about half an inch high. I snowplowed most of the way down but survived to do two or three runs.

That evening my parents and I were in Agora (the level-floored theater and meeting place of the Club) for a cocktail. Muscles aching, I told of my adventures and was advised by several men I did not know that I should take a hot bath! I now stick to cross country and did that at least once on the golf course of the Club.

Our experiences at the Club were all good. We stayed until it closed and then followed, as closely as we could from Connecticut, the hopes of a new owner and renovation. I knew the outcome of those plans but March 2000 was the first time I had seen that side of the Mirror Lake with no building on it. It seemed strange to walk up to where the front entrance had been and pick up shards of French plate glass that hold so many memories.

I have read with great interest David Ackerman's Lake Placid Club, An Illustrated History. Two of his statements seem particularly important to me; "the success of a place of accommodation depends upon its employees", and "More than just the buildings and related amenities, it was the people of the community who made it [the Club] possible."

As I walked along Main St. and talked to people in the shops, if the Club was mentioned, invariably the response was, "I worked there," or "My mother worked in the kitchen," or "I was a Rolls and Relish girl!" Those stories are worth telling and both honor the employees of the Club and record the story of the Lake Placid Club from the perspective of the people who made it work, its employees.

THE RESEARCH PROCESS

My parents, Gordon K. and Marguerite C. Campbell, and I had first eaten dinner at the Club, according to Mother's notes and collected ephemera, in February 1957 and stayed as introduced guests sponsored by Albert T. Dewey of Manchester, Conn., always in February, 1961, '63, '64, '66, '68, '69 (I took two ski lessons; there were 18 inches of snow), '72 and until 1980.

I read Ackerman's Illustrated History of the Club which revived my own memories.

I saw that an equally valid history of the Club would be the stories of the people who worked inside the Club, not the famous, not the wealthy, not the ones who arrived by train for the season. My focus would be the people from "overtown" who seasonally and year-round made the grounds attractive, instructed the sports activities, cooked the food, served it, and did the dishes; and the Front bellboys and clerks seen and the Power House engineers not seen.

I started research at the New York State Library in Albany, where Melvil Dewey, Club founder (best known as the creator of the Dewey Decimal System for libraries), had been Librarian of the State of New York from 1889 to 1905. I then went to the National Archives Branch in Pittsfield, Mass. There I found New York State and United States Census data for Essex County, Town of North Elba, and the listings of the employees residing at the Club by name, age, race, ability to read, write and speak English, and more importantly, by job: hostler (one who takes care of horses), teamster (one who drives horses), painter, fireman, laundress, waitress.

I wrote to Town and Village Historian Mary MacKenzie, who was cautious but welcoming, "...virtually every other citizen either worked at the Club for varying periods or had a relative who did. A book about their personal experiences could well be of value. My initial reaction is that it may be a bit late to try to gather significant material. The majority of those who worked at the Club during its 85 year history are long gone. Few first hand accounts would be available...I certainly do not want to discourage you or dampen your ardor. As I see it, the only possible way you can determine the wisdom of such a book is to first come up here and conduct some exploratory interviews."

My first call to the Lake Placid Library was greeted enthusiastically by Linda Blair, who immediately said, "I was a Rolls and Relish girl!" She created the first list of people for me to interview and she put up my poster announcing when I would be at the Library. On one of their most hectic Library days (the then annual Book Sale), Children's Librarian Louise Patenelli simply said, "Use my desk" and former Club employees were sent down to me in the Children's Room: caddies, laundry workers, chef.

Lee Manchester of the *Lake Placid News* interviewed me and ran the article that resulted in e-mails from 80-year-olds and many others. Adults called their parents and grandparents who had worked at the Club and I heard from or called the relatives. A Club member wrote a waitress she had known 60 years before; and the waitress responded from Pennsylvania, and her friend, also a waitress, from Michigan.

Soon I was told the Club archives had been given to the Library but only a Finding Aid had been created of the material. Cataloging would come later and by then the snowbank would have melted in front of the door where the cartons were stored so I could see the actual documents. One extended stay in the archives got me through 22 cartons I selected from the Finding Aid and I had to strictly discipline myself NOT to read everything. Keep your focus, Barbara!

During this time period, Mary MacKenzie retired as historian and her files were moved to the Lake Placid Library so I had access to them, too.

Older information came from Club Notes written by Melvil Dewey, the writing tone consistent for 30 years – enthusiastic, proud, the consummate salesman for a place he loved. Yes, maybe the writing was a tad overstated!

I returned to Lake Placid on my fall, spring and summer semester breaks from the University of Connecticut and my contacts grew. Every interview ended with, "You should talk to..." Some were formal interviews with two tape recorders, the tapes later transcribed. Other interviews were conducted at Town Hall, where the senior citizens have lunch; in lovely living rooms of Lake Placid homes; in the Golf House; on the front steps of the Library as a former chef was cooking hot dogs; on the shore of Lake Placid itself, notebook resting on the fender of a carpenter's truck on a beautiful spring day; and at Uihlein Mercy Center, where some older Club employees lived.

Essential to the research process were breakfasts of mixed berry crepes at Aroma Round and walking around Mirror Lake (2.7 miles) in the evening. It's a level walk that ends with a choice of fine restaurants on Main Street, Lake Placid.

My iBook computer, printer and I spent Thanksgiving 2001 at Mohonk Mountain House, New Paltz, N.Y. It is a Victorian hotel owned and operated by the Smiley family since 1869 (older than the Club!) My mother and I had vacationed there and agreed it was the closest to being at the Club that we had found. Melvil Dewey actually recommended Mohonk Mountain House to his members in Club Notes May 1921. I hope the atmosphere rubbed off into my writing. I know I was so absorbed I missed going down to afternoon tea one day! Remembering my chapter on chambermaids, I was careful to put the "Please Make Up This Room" tag on the doorknob of my room so that that chambermaid would know I was up and out and she would be able to come in and cross one more room off her daily list.

First readings of the manuscript have been done by Therese Patnode, Lake Placid Library Director, by Cliff Auctor in Ellington, Conn. who knows the Adirondacks, and Elisa McCarthy in West Hartford, Conn. who has never been to Lake Placid but kept telling me, "I need description." I kept telling her, "There will be pictures!" My cat vacationed at her home while I was on research trips to Lake Placid – the most memorable trip being on Christmas Day 2002 driving into a blizzard all the way north from Connecticut. Elisa's reading of the final text was careful, helpful and challenging.

Special thanks to Siobhan Dugan, my editor, who marked my technical mistakes, got involved in the subject matter and asked clarifying questions by e-mail and in the hard copy text.

The professionalism of all the librarians of the Lake Placid Library was so helpful. They all understand the research process and know the material they have to offer in the library and online. The writing desk I used overlooks Mirror Lake and has a view of Whiteface. Better than that, however, was the response of Librarian Patty Perez, "Yes, I'll canoe Mirror Lake with you and do you want to go for a swim?" Afterwards we sat at lakeshore in the Library's Adirondack chairs and looked to where the Lake Placid Club used to be, the grassy area on the east shore.

INTRODUCTION

Up the Northway, on your way from Albany to the Canadian border, take Exit 30 through Keene Valley and drive along the Cascade Lakes. Coming into the village of Lake Placid on Route 73, go past the sign to the Lake Placid Historical Museum in the train station, and the Lake Placid News. Come to a traffic light. Turning right leads to Whiteface Mountain, but a left puts you on Main Street (also known as Mirror Lake Drive).

Town Hall is across Main Street from Lake Placid High School, which is next door to the 1980 and 1932 Olympic Ice Arenas. The Post Office is at the turn in Main Street. You have passed resorts and hotels, with more to come along the shore of Mirror Lake. Nestled among the shops are the bank, the lovely Lake Placid Library and restaurants.

On a quiet June evening, just before school is out, you can have dinner outdoors on the edge of Mirror Lake, watch a lone double kayak pace the lake as the carillon from St. Eustace Episcopal Church joins the restaurant music. The annual Whiteface Mountain Uphill Run is over and the Horse Show is about to usher in the summer season.

Across Mirror Lake, on the east shore, there is a long 10-to-12 foot high stone wall beyond which lies a green expanse of lawn.

Within the village, in some of the antique shops, you will occasionally find a piece of ephemera called Club Notes. Written in "simpler speling" developed by Melvil Dewey, Club Notes tell part of the story of the Lake Placid Club started by Dewey that, for 85 years, sat on that grassy lawn above the curving stonewall by Mirror Lake across from the village.

All that is there now are shards of the French plate glass from the windows that lined the lobby and lounge. Until January 2002 there was a brown wooden theater building with pillars called Agora, pronounced, "Ag-ra." Behind Agora, the swimming pool lay dry and chapel windows above it once filled with Tiffany glass were boarded up. Connected to the theater was a brick, 1920s hotel building, also called Agora, now closed, and torn down.

Had you turned up the hill by Town Hall between 1895 and 1980, and gone a block or two, you would have turned right at the stone pillar announcing "Lake Placid Club, Entrance, Private." When you drove under the portico you were greeted by the bellmen of the Lake Placid Club. They would welcome you to a large, rambling Adirondack-style property that regularly accommodated 1,200 members and guests (1,602 during the 1932 Olympics). During peak periods 1,100 employees were employed from the Tri Lakes area (Lake Placid, Saranac Lake, and Tupper Lake), and seasonally, from colleges across the United States.

The Club, with its 40-plus farms and dairies, lake access, golf courses, power house, Mt. Whitney Ski Lodge, general store, dining rooms, fire patrol, and post office was a self- sufficient year-round institution. The Lake Placid Company governed the policies and managed the property while Club members oversaw social activities and membership that provided financial support. But the Club employees made it happen, made it pleasant, made it a welcoming place to return to year after year.

Imagine, if you will, making sure there are clean sheets and pillowcases available twice a week for some 500 beds. Imagine preparing prime rib for 1,200 hungry people. Imagine decorating those lounges and rooms with Club-grown flowers. Imagine being the caddy who walks the golf courses surrounded by magnificent views of the Sentinel Mountain range. And imagine relaxing between your shifts as a waitress, with friends and a bowl of rich Club creamery ice cream!

Picture yourself now in an Adirondack lawn chair, or curled up in front of the lobby fireplace. Perhaps you're being served hot chocolate on the deck at the Ski Lodge at Mt. Whitney, or relaxing after the 18th hole. Listen to the stories of the employees of the former Lake Placid Club who knew everyone by name and who were there at the Club to make your stay pleasant and memorable.

CHAPTER 1

Welcome to the Club
Front, Please, and the Naked Lady

Club members and guests had arrived when they drove or were chauffered, up through the driveway by the stone pillar sedately stating, "Lake Placid Club Entrance Private." Under the portico in winter, bellmen in brown wool overcoats noted the six inches of ice on headlights. These formed as members came through the winter storms by the Cascade Lakes where ice-blue icicles lined the side banks of the road.

Winter or summer, the greeting was warm. Members and guests were expected, their rooms ready and all was right with the world. The greeters, the bellmen, knew they had the best job at the Club. They met everyone, were the highest-ranking employees at the service level, made the most money, and worked the best hours.

Club Bel servis (Dewey's Simplified spelling) manual mandated in 1918 that: "The ideal bellboy is of medium height and weight, with no oddities of manner or physical deformity. He has a calm, well-ordered mind that grasps instructions easily and he performs his duties quietly, quickly, politely and correctly."

In 1922, the contract of Edmund S. Woodard as a bell boy specified he agreed to work 10 hours a day "or in an emergency as many hours as my department deems necessary, including Sunday." For this he was paid $1.90 a day, out of which Woodard paid the Lake Placid Company for board, room, laundry, traveling and other personal expenses. He was to abstain wholly from liquor, tobacco, vulgarity, profanity or gambling even for the smallest stakes. He agreed to pay reduced prices for livery and cars, boats, golf and laundry. He was to secure harmony and good will, and obey fire rules strictly and participate in fire drills. His contract could be canceled on two days' notice.

In 1936-38, Cal Wilson was a bellhop whose duties included handling Special Delivery mail. He enjoyed performing whatever services people required. That could be delivering papers, carrying luggage or walking overtown to the village to run errands. The Special Delivery service involved delivering letters directly to guest rooms or, if they weren't in their rooms, putting a notice on the door to come down to the U. S. Post Office in the Club.

Bellmen were the front-line messengers between the outside world and Club members. Bellmen received slips of paper from the Front Desk with the names of each guest and had to be able to recognize all members and their guests and greet them by name, correctly pronounced. Malcolm Alford apprenticed for the position by delivering newspapers to the 90 or so cottages of the Club. In his second year, his responsibilities increased and he delivered telegrams. By the end of his apprenticeship he knew every member and where they lived for the season in the Club.

Bellmen escorted guests to their room, prompting them as the elevator arrived at their floor, "to the right, please." Guests entered the room first and luggage was placed where requested. Bellmen then inspected the room and reported any missing toilet supplies or burned out light bulbs immediately to the housekeeper.

Bellmen worked a long and a short day, from 7 a.m. to noon, returning at 6 p.m. and working staggered hours until 11 p.m. for the long day. The short day was noon to 6 p.m. This was done seven days a week during the summer. In the late 1940s, the pay was about seventeen dollars a week, 10 percent retained by the Club until after Labor Day to ensure employees did not quit before the end of summer. Most guests stayed until the last week of August or Labor Day weekend.

The Club didn't exactly provide the Bellmen's uniforms. Again according to Bel servis, a brown suit made to order from measurements was furnished each bellboy and charged to him at wholesale cost (about $25), along with white starched collars, brown neckties, brown or dark socks, brown shoes with rubber heels (one pair of heels each season was furnished by the Club), a rain coat marked plainly with the owner's name. Uniforms in good condition would be bought back at a fair price.

Numbered badges always worn on duty were 50 cents, refunded upon their return. Pass keys were held by bellmen on a 25 cent deposit.

There was pride in holding the position of bellman, as well as bearing the responsibility of upholding Club standards. If a member or guest was on the putting green or listening to the Rochester Philharmonic live on the front lawn and received a phone call or message, the Front Desk gave the message to the bellman who would quietly inform the member of the message. Paging began at the Front Desk. The name was to be spoken in an inquiring tone of voice in public rooms, porches and amongst groups of people at tennis matches or rink activities. In the Dining Room the head waitress was the only person who could give permission for paging while members and guests were eating.

Bellmen stood erect in the military "at ease" position and Club members were quick to criticize "sloughiness." Bellmen never showed impatience when a member or guest was making a request. They knew the elderly often needed special guidance in or to public rooms. They passed behind, never in front of, guests. They were instructed to give only the cheaper stationery to children or employees.

Bellmen were instructed how to place the 12", 18" or 24" logs properly in fireplaces, with air spaces, on a three inch bed of ashes, omitting paper or shavings under the kindling until the fire was to be lit. More wood was added to keep the fire blazing. Discarded guest newspapers were saved for starting fires. Newspapers and books with the Club library marks, however, were to be returned to the library.

In the early days, according to Frances Silleck, guests were met at the train station by Club horses and sleigh driven by her father, Frederick H. Douglass. No horses, however, were allowed to stand at Clubhouse entrances longer than necessary for arrivals and departures (due to their natural habits.) As automobiles became more common, members' chauffeurs would help their passengers out of the car at the Clubhouse entrance, the car would be unloaded by bellmen, and the chauffeur would park the car and go to his Club accommodations. Or perhaps a Club limousine, a DeSoto driven by Ray McIntyre, would pick the members up at the train. McIntrye drove limousines while he was in college for three summers and one fall. He chauffeured Lowell Thomas and Gene Tunney (the prize fighter who defeated Jack Dempsey in 1926). Guests would be chauffeured to the Lake Placid train station and also to New York City, Boston or the train station in Westport, N. Y. He would also pick the waitresses of the Club up at 6:15 a.m. Sundays and take them to Mass at St. Agnes Roman Catholic Church.

Bellmen handled ice calls (deliveries of a large container of ice for private parties) and delivery of pitchers of ice water (the cleaning of those pitchers carefully prescribed.) One afternoon during his apprenticeship, Malcolm Alford recalls they were short of bellmen and extremely busy. "I was handling an ice call when the head bellman called me over to find a person and have them come to the Front Desk. The person was a newly arrived guest unfamiliar in name or face to me. As I approached Agora Lounge, I quietly began paging the men seated and reading, "Paging Mr. Briefcase. Mr. Briefcase, please" (the real identity still discretely protected).

"Finally one gentleman raised his hand and signaled for me to come over. 'Are you paging Mr. Portfolio?'

"I was deadly afraid, and with good reason, that I would be dismissed from the Club. This was an extremely serious blunder. Fortunately, he took it in good humor and all passed."

Alford recalled how the bellmen hated rainy days. "The young ladies would be off the golf courses and tennis courts and usually lounging around in the area known as Agora Lounge. It was a rather large area with overstuffed chairs and small side tables located immediately next to the soda fountain. The rich ice cream and milk, fresh from the Lake Placid Club's own dairy farms, made heavenly milk shakes. I can still taste them!

"There was a fairly well supported history of the girls costing bellmen their jobs by placing them in compromising positions. The guests and help were always non-fraternizing. We could not be caught talking to them in any kind of a personal manner or even arrange to meet them overtown. (The Club was on the east shore of Mirror Lake, the town, or more accurately the village of Lake Placid, is across the Lake on the west shore.) It was extremely important that you maintained a purely professional manner. The members would not allow any flexibility on this issue. For instance, if you and a guest were heading toward the same door you could never win the race to the door. Seems simple but it cost at least one bellman his job.

"The girls had some kind of an unwritten game whose object was to get a bellman, houseman or waiter in trouble. More than once, I was on an ice call to the Forest East Suites using the elevator when, just before the door would close, a female Club member would step into the elevator. I would press her floor number and quickly exit. I had heard stories of guests yelling in the elevator and claiming that the employee had made some overt overtures toward them. The elevator entrance was right at the Agora Lounge and the girls would giggle when they saw me exit. Probably an over-reaction but I couldn't afford to risk it."

Celebrities, such as Arthur Godfrey (the CBS radio and TV personality), violinist Fritz Kreisler, and prominent businessmen such as Sherman Billingsley, owner of the Stork Club in New York City, frequented the Club. Billingsley would come up for about two weekends but his wife and three daughters spent the summer. About 1949, the girls were Shermaine, age 3; Barbara, 15; and an older daughter in her 20s.

"Little Shermaine would come running down the lobby, jump in my lap and beg me to unlock the shuffleboard, " Alford recalls. "I would take her to the shuffleboard area and play one quick game while her nanny watched. This was a ritual along with the delivery to her room, everyday, of an airmail letter from Mr. Billingsley containing a brief message and a crisp one dollar bill. While Shermaine was opening the mail, the nanny would tip me one dollar for the delivery.

"I was off duty and happened to be home when the head bellman, Walter Whitney, called and said I had to come over to work immediately. When I arrived I found out that the Billingsleys were checking out and had asked for me in particular. This was unusual. (Bellmen were supposed to be of service, not treated as individuals.) It took almost the entire bellstaff to check them out. The Club limos were packed to the brim and running constantly to the train station and back.

"Finally the family came out. Mr. Billingsley came over to me and handed me a small oblong box, shook my hand and said something about how much Shermaine appreciated the extra attention. He said for me to bring my mom to the city and there would be reservations for the two of us at the Stork Club any time we wanted. The box contained a tie, solid blue with a gold chain running down the center and a sculpted stork on the end. The inscription on the back read, 'Compliments of the Stork Club.' I am sure there was a large blanket tip left; my share I cannot remember."

The Club porter was under contract to get Pullman and railroad tickets for members and guests. The Club advanced the capital (sometimes $3,000 to $5,000 a day), and did so with no charge to members but, "The Porter's salary depends on his NOT accepting a single tip during the year. He would render the best service in his power with absolute fairness to all because it is a pleasure as well as a duty and for that no tip can ever be taken," stated Club Notes. Other benefits did accrue to some of those in service at the Club, according to Bel servis manuals. The majority of Club bellboys were earnest young men, trying to help themselves through college and Club members often became interested in them and rendered substantial aid which led to desirable and permanent positions.

Bellman Robert Blanchard, in the early 1940s, remembered waiting for the train to come morning and evening, and being busy with check-ins and check-outs. He, too, did ice calls in the evening. No liquor was sold in the Club then but bellmen did set up for huge cocktail parties whenever members requested them. "Anything the guests want," was the attitude, even taking shoes overtown to get them fixed.

One night CBS news commentator Lowell Thomas was broadcasting from the Club. An urgent telegram came for him. The bell captain told Blanchard, "You have to deliver this immediately to Mr. Thomas. Don't give it to anyone but Mr. Thomas."

The guy by the curtain tried to stop him and said to Blanchard, "I'll take it."

Blanchard said, "I was directed to give it directly to Mr. Thomas." Blanchard recalled he succeeded but almost fainted dead away when Lowell Thomas started carrying on a short conversation with him.

In 1946, Harry Purchase went to the Club wanting a bellman's job. An elevator operator had just quit and Harry was asked, "Can you start this afternoon?" Harry, correctly reading the offer behind the question, accepted the up and down job and became a bellman the next summer. Bellmen were familiar with the entire range of duties; including elevator operation.

Dr. George Hart's experience as a bellhop was memorable. He had to deliver flowers to a lady's room. He walked in and she was lying in bed stark naked. Startled, Dr. Hart said, "Oh, excuse me!"

She said, "Oh, that's all right. I thought you were the garage man coming to fix my car," Dr. Hart recalled.

Bell captains supervised the work of bellboys and the head bellman kept them all in line. That line was literal. Bellmen took orders in rotation returning quickly to their place at the end of the line. Should unbidden guests arrive on the premises not recognized by front clerk or room clerk, the head bellman (or superintendent of service) was instructed to greet the stranger by saying he would be glad to find his friends if they would provide the head bellman the name. Such delicate situations were handled with dignity, tact and courtesy. All outside messengers were intercepted and their errand given to a bellboy. Outside messengers did not wander Club grounds.

Front Desk

Anne Huttlinger worked for Northeast Airlines in the middle of WW II in Boston. The station manager would walk through the office saying, "I've got to find someone to go to Presque Isle, Maine. Anne would say, "I'll go." He at first thought it was no place for a young girl but then agreed she could go, and she loved it. She later worked for United Airlines in Seattle. When she was furloughed, she returned home to Boston and took Gregg shorthand and typing. She learned a little bit but took dictation according to her own devises.

Her pioneering spirit kicked in again as she thought it would be fun to work at a ski resort, so she went to Lake Placid. She was hired in January 1948, married in October 1950 and worked until June 1951. The first winter she had a "dumb little job in the sports office." It was the base for ski instructors and she took messages for them. They would come to the office after skiing was over and, indoors, try to teach Anne how to ski. She then worked for Dannie Nelson, reservations manager, "who never got going until 4 p.m. and then everything had to be done."

The same people would reserve the same rooms, usually July 4th to Labor Day, and made the next year's reservation when they left. Anne worked with Lucille Packer, daughter of Samuel Packer, Club manager in the late `30s and `40s. The correspondence they handled on electric typewriters was voluminous.

Godfrey Dewey, son of Melvil and Annie Dewey, tried unsuccessfully to take his father's place at the Club after Melvil died in 1931. He was his father's son but loyalty to a man the stature and nature of Melvil Dewey did not transfer. Explicit instructions

Godfrey gave for transcribing his dictation, however, were definitely of the period..

"I usually dictate break for a paragraph, curves and curves closed for parentheses, quotes and quotes closed for quotations.

"Stationary to be used will be dictated, together with instructions for any extra carbon copies, in addition to the usual yellow file copy. Extra thin copies are to be inserted between the original and file copy."

One of the Club employees was a teacher who worked summers at the Club. Once he looked at the list of incoming guests, found a single female name and asked the front desk clerks expectantly, "What's she like?" He was be told, "She's adorable" and he got his hopes up. In truth, she was an adorable little old lady.

Anne and Jerry Huttlinger broke Club standards, which frowned on an employee's dating a junior member (son of a member). On a date they would go down to the barber shop in the Club and talk to George. "George was from Greece, spoke English, sort of, was an old grouch but liked us," Anne Huttlinger said. Gentlemen members would put their shoes outside their door at night, George would pick them up, polish and return them. He tried to get Anne and Jerry to go into the business, "You could earn a lot of money!" It was thought that George through his employment at the Club supported a whole village in Greece. People gave him used clothes that he packaged and sent to home. George had to stop polishing shoes because his hands became allergic to the shoe polish and eventually he did return to Greece.

Anne and Jerry Huttlinger were married in October 1950. At the time, working women had to hide the fact that they were pregnant and leave work when they "showed." Club manager Jack Watt was upset about it but Anne was a good worker, couldn't be replaced and worked until June. Her son, John, was born July 1951.

At various times, there were three Front Desks, the earliest at Lakeside (or Laksyd - Dewey's spelling) last used for members and guests in 1931 and demolished in 1946. Lakeside Clubhouse consisted of several buildings cobbled together, and including Bonniblink, the first building the Deweys took title to. Another Front Desk was in Theanoguen, where Raymond McIntyre, in the late 1950s worked long and short days keeping the books and the accounting sheet for each day. The third Front Desk and the one most would remember today was in Forest and faced Mirror Lake.

CHAPTER 2

Housekeeping, Please and the Dog Chewed the Book

A chambermaid had to have a lively interest in the people she worked for, had to know when to mother them and when to let her personality shine through her efficiency. This was still clearly evident when, at age 95, Blanche McCasland was interviewed in 2000. She enjoyed every minute of her 27 years at the Club and enjoyed all those people she met. Her husband didn't want her to work but her sons were in the armed services and everyone was working at the Club.

McCasland reminisced about Pat Boone with Arthur Godfrey at the Club, Fritz Kreisler who wanted to play for the house but his wife wouldn't let him, and baritone Vaughn Monroe who invited her back to hear him sing "White Christmas." Eunice Kennedy was on McCasland's floor, but in 1965, Robert Kennedy, who stayed at the Golden Arrow Hotel in Lake Placid, made her move her family out of the Club because the Club didn't accept Jews or Blacks. There were the Russians who came for the FISU games (World University Winter Games, Feb. 25-Mar. 5, 1972, of the International University Sports Federation) and kept dried fish on the window sill. The Pulitzers confided in McCasland that their name was Pul-it-zer not Pil-it-zer "as everybody calls us." The Pulitzers bought land in Ausable for a summer home. It was part of McCasland's grandfather's property.

Remembering how the guests arranged their belongings was the chambermaid's responsibility. McCasland would write down where guests put their things so when they came back the next season, everything would be in place. One member had his clothes on a rack in the next room and asked her for an extra sheet to cover the clothes. She told him, "If you look on top of the rack, the sheet is there." He had also asked for a sheet the previous year.

Chambermaid Directions were published in 1918 and 1929. Chambermaids were encouraged to take pleasure in doing their work well. They were encouraged to be quiet and courteous, honest and neat and wear rubber heels! A small portion of their detailed instructions follows:

Maids had to report any evidence of mice and insect pests (bed bugs, water bugs, bristle tails) to the housekeeper at once. She depended on her maids to keep the house entirely free of vermin.

Maids' equipment included regular cleaning implements plus a painter's brush for wicker furniture, button hook for cleaning waste pipes, and wooden sticks for corners. Carpet sweepers were used on large rugs with the maids careful to watch for small items such as jewelry. Waste from the carpet sweeper was to be burned.

If storms came up, maids were to "close at once all windows on your floor into which rain might beat."

Closets were cleaned before rooms. Placement of items on commodes was prescribed; pitcher and basin in center, shaving mug and toothbrush holder to the left back, glass and soap dish, right back.

Items on desks were never to be rearranged; clean blotters were supplied in brown, gray, or green as harmonized with the room. Ash trays were added in 1929.

Drawer liners were saved and cut to fit the wastepaper baskets. Contents of wastepaper baskets were examined for things of value to the guest or the Club.

Feather dusters were never to be used, hemmed cheese cloth was much better.

After 6:30 p.m., beds were to be opened and bathrooms checked for neatness and change of towels if "clearly soiled."

Fireplace hearths were to be swept and ashes put well back from the front of andirons. Mayflower stoves were to be dusted and brass polished. Housemen occasionally blackened the stoves.

Floors were waxed, varnished or tiled, all with separate cleaning instructions for each. Sapolio, a cleanser, was used on tile floors when needed.

In kitchenettes, silver was polished weekly.

Maids were told report at once to the housekeeper any evidence of alcohol or other types of burners for curling hair or heating food. An electric hot plate could be rented for heating a baby's food; and nothing else!

Maids counted and listed all soiled linens from their rooms daily. Linens spotted, torn or wrinkled on opening were taken to the Linen Room for repairs and the housekeeper was to be notified so she could correct such work.

Floors were dry mopped before rugs were spread. Wet mops were washed and dried. "No unpleasant odor should be left in them."

A special brush of hair was used behind, under and between the sections of radiators weekly. Floor registers were lifted out weekly and cleaned; "wiping down into pipes as far as can be reached."

Ice boxes were cleaned with ammonia. If the ice was dirty or had sawdust on it (it was lake ice from the previous winter stored in saw dust in the ice house), the ice was replaced.

Long-staying guests used the large sized Palmolive soap but transients were given the small size. Bath tubs were stocked with Ivory soap.

Stairs were swept with whisk brooms and dust pans, with balustrades and each step dusted. Both sides and corners of brooms were to be used by turning the broom occasionally. Vacuum cleaners were used at least once a month in 1929.

The mouthpiece of the telephone was wiped each day and disinfected when the occupant of the room changed.

Three fresh face towels and two bath towels were changed every morning in single rooms; five face and three bath towels in double rooms. Towels in public lavatories were changed four times a day.

Window shades were wiped on both sides with a long handled brush. "In very warm weather, judgement must be used as to shutting out the glare and heat of midday; but in Adirondack climate there are few days when it is not more comfortable to have the rooms flooded with sunshine, and this is the Club custom."

Windows were washed with warm water and ammonia. "Paint spatters may be...rubbed with the edge of a cent, fly specks with a bit of wood."

Cleaning work must be planned for when the guests were out of their rooms. Beds were opened and baths done first. In the bathroom, toilets were cleaned first and rinsed with scalding water. Tubs were washed with a cloth and Ivory soap. Bon Ami cleanser was used if soap scum remained. A fresh apron was put on for bedmaking, dusting and general cleaning.

Clean glass towels were used for washing drinking glasses, mugs and holders. Silver polish was used on faucets. Each bathroom had an Onliwon toilet paper fixture (it dispensed only one sheet of toilet paper at a time; a frugal dispensor) that was kept filled and an extra roll left on the shelf for emergencies.

Rooms were aired and windows opened top and bottom. Mattresses were turned end to end or side to side each morning. Bottom sheets were spread right side up and square corners turned. Upper sheets were spread wrong side up, broad hem at top. The upper sheet was folded over edges of blankets at top using at least one to two yards of upper sheet to protect the blanket.

Single beds were changed once a week, double beds twice a week when occupied by two people, using one fresh sheet each time.

Guests' clothing left scattered was to be hung in the closet, shoes and slippers put away.

Longer and harder parts of irregular cleaning work were divided among different rooms on different days so the work load was evenly distributed. Consultations were held with the housekeeper for scheduling assistance.

"A personal interest in having everything complete and in order, is unconsciously felt by the arriving guest as a welcome."

Thus were set the standards for care of the chambers of the Club.

Ida L. Cooley was a chambermaid taking care of the 16 rooms in Theanoguen and eight rooms in a cottage. She worked 8 a.m. to 1 p.m. and 6 p.m. to 8 p.m. In the summer of 1938 for 31 days she earned $1.74 a day minus $.90 a day for meals. Room was included. In 1939 her daily rate of pay went up to $2.70.

Mrs. Dow, housekeeping head, took notes also when guests lived in the cottages. There it was possible for guests to have their own refrigerator, furniture and other household items brought out for their season's stay and put in storage when they left.

Blanche McCasland worked year round, did cleaning for conventions in the off season but she said she really enjoyed the summer people. She worked the third floor of Agora. A couple from her floor were invited by friends to stay on the fourth floor. They went up for one night but came right back to the third floor and "said they didn't feel at home up there."

A couple once had a car wreck on their way up to the Club. The wife was bruised and had taken to her bed. McCasland told her she needed moist heat and wet towels for her with hot water. McCasland's family had two race horses, so she knew about horse liniment, brought some in and rubbed it on the woman. When Dr. Bergamini came, he told Blanche the moist heat was just what the woman needed and the horse liniment was good, too, except for the smell.

Honesty was paramount for chambermaids. McCasland recalled that once a man and his wife had two rooms. When McCasland made the bed, she found his wallet under his pillow. She made the bed and put the wallet back on the pillow. He realized at breakfast he didn't have his wallet. He was very grateful to her because the money for the whole summer was in it.

Agnes Howe was a chambermaid for 26 years from 1936 to 1962. She worked April to October and was assigned to three of the cottages. She would work 8 a.m. to 1 p.m. and come back to turn down beds from 6:30 to 8:30 p.m. She cleaned the rooms (a vacuum cleaner was in each cottage) and made beds. Towels were changed daily and again at night if they were wet. Howe was placed in charge of young chambermaids, some of whom didn't know how to make a bed. She wore a blue uniform with a white apron and got a clean one once a week or more often if she asked for one.

Leona Preston was a chambermaid in the 1940s, worked in Agora and said the Club was a good place to work.

May Lawrence, Village Treasurer Virginia Gilmore's grandmother, worked as a chambermaid at the Golfery (which had rooms for young single businessmen having short vacations) when she was in her 70s. She was a very proper person and came home one day to say that while she was there, one of the young men stepped out of the shower with nothing on. Asked what she did, she said, "I just kept about my work!"

Dr. George Hart, in the 1920s, and Robert Blanchard, in the 1940s, were housemen. For one season Dr. Hart helped clean the cottages and get them ready for summer rental. Blanchard came to work at 6 a.m., did early morning cleaning and if a guest wanted a chair moved out and another put in, he did it. He found there was more money to make working on the golf course.

Chambermaids were helpful to the Club librarian who reported in December 1962 that 1,013 books had been checked out that month. "Over three cold days most of my new magazines were stolen. Some were returned to the Club library by chambermaids when guests checked out. Rental books were left with bellboys to return without paying the rental!"

Special library collections included "Comparative Christianity," Adirondack books and abolitionist John Brown books. The library was a quiet, pleasant space with a fireplace and a good children's collection. Cornelia Bonsignore worked summers and during school vacations in the library and children's library.

The librarian's report carefully mentioned all the reasons for continuing to support the library; a place of enjoyment for children, assistance for teachers, resource for Northwoods students and coordination with conventions.

In February of 1961, the librarian continued in her report, 95 western novels and 65 mystery novels no longer being read by members were sent to Sunmount Veterans Hospital in Tupper Lake. The use of children's books ran higher than usual due to unfavorable weather and lack of snow.

During April 1961, students at Northwoods School, the private school that was sponsored by the Club, were doing special reports.

During May 1962 at two big conventions (School Supervisors and Rotary) there were frequent remarks about the joy of finding one room free of talk and free from smoke. Five books were borrowed from the State Library in Albany to fill special requests. College students wanted language books, science books and literary reading. An exhibit was set up on the country where the next Rotary International convention would be.

In July 1962, 2,032 books were checked out and the call for books for school reading lists was very heavy. The librarian did some extensive research for a teacher who was making lesson plans for grade school work on soil and water conservation.

In August 1962, "Mrs Sherrerd's dog chewed up one of my most popular rental books so she had to be charged for it," the librarian wrote.

CHAPTER 3

Strings, Stems and a Moose-size Wreath

Mountains, forests and the lake set the ambiance outdoors but what better way to create an indoor atmosphere than with music and flowers!

Since 1917 there was a tradition of the Boston Symphony Orchestra summering at the Club, but in the 1930s the BSO switched to Tanglewood at Stockbridge in the Berkshires of Massachusetts for their summer concerts. For a few years after the switch, Boston Symphony members continued to come to the Club but had to have three weeks off for Tanglewood concerts.

At Thanksgiving 1938 Paul White, who played second violin with the Rochester Philharmonic and was assistant conductor and a teacher at the Eastman School of Music of the University of Rochester, was invited to bring a small group of musicians to the Club to audition. At Eastman, White conducted the junior and senior orchestras (each with from 80 to 100 pieces) and, as assistant conductor, supervised the children's concert, ballet concert and some regular concerts. The Club liked what they heard and in the summer of 1939 the Sinfonietta started an almost 40-year summer relationship with the Club. (Unlike many names of places and buildings around the Club, such as Squealery for children's playground, Maidery and Mennery for dormitories, "Sinfonietta" is not unique to the Club and simply means a little symphony of 12 to 19 members.) Only for a few summers during WW II did they not play. Paul White planned the programs that were similar and pleasant from year to year.

Dr. White knew the van Hoesin family as his three daughters were close to young David van Hoesin's age. One daughter played French horn. They had no one to play bass so Dr. White suggested to van Hoesin's father, "Why don't you bring David up?" He played strings in 1947 and then filled out the woodwinds becoming principal oboeist. At the time the Club was going full strength, the general store and meat market, laundry and dry cleaning, tailor and barber shop were bustling making it an exciting venue for a young man.

The work week? Sinfonietta musicians had Mondays off. Tuesdays it was the children's concert. Wednesday afternoon featured a one hour concert outdoors by the putting green "when the blue-haired ladies had tea." [It was a stylish rinse so the yellow of the ladies' white hair didn't show. These ladies were not countercultural] Thursday morning was a chamber music concert sometimes with Carl Lamson, pianist for Fritz Kreisler, sometimes strings, sometimes a woodwind quartet. Thursday afternoon was the putting green concert (held in Forest Music Room when it rained). Saturday morning was rehearsal with Dr. White, a very gentle man. Sometimes it was just for a half hour and much of that time was spent making sure they all had the right music. Saturday night was a "serious" concert in Forest Music Room after the children's dancing party and before the big dance at which the Club dance band played; and Sunday night was another "serious" concert in Agora Theater that several hundred attended.

The nine-or-ten week plus two day season was much heavier than the six week season the Sinfonietta now plays in Lake Placid in the Paul White Music Shell on Main St. Musicians were then paid $55 a week plus Club privileges.

From the Boston Symphony years, an extensive library of music was developed at the Club. When the Sinfonietta played their last

Club concert in 1976 (due to the situation at the Club and the coming of television), there was a night caravan of cars when the music was moved from the Club to the Lake Placid Arts Center.

Small movie theaters had small orchestras. David van Hoesin's father played in the Picadelli Theater in Rochester. These small orchestras needed classical music arranged for small groups, some of which was published by Carl Fisher. In the late days of the silent films, while the reels were being changed, the orchestra pit in some theaters would rise, a concert was played and the pit lowered for the second reel. Music for these theater orchestras was perfect for an orchestra the size of the Sinfonietta.

Since adding to the music library was expensive, musicians such as David van Hoesin cross-cued the music. For example, van Hoesin said if the piece needed two flutes but the orchestra had one flute, cross-cueing the music meant writing the second flute part for clarinet or oboe. Beethoven's 8th can be cross-cued, Brahms doesn't work and the bigger Beethoven works sound strange, so they weren't done. The Sinfonietta played a whole Wagner concert with its 12 musicians. In the music collection now at the Lake Placid Center for the Arts, there is also French music with names of early players stamped on it.

From a generous supporter, the Sinfonietta did receive a grant for the upkeep of their music library and they were able to get Broadway show tunes.

Some members of the Sinfonietta who were just out of the Eastman School trained at the Club and went on to significant positions. The violin concert master at the Metropolitan Opera in New York City came from the Sinfonietta, as did the Met's principal second violinist. One alumnus went to the New York Philharmonic.

The Sinfonietta musicians were conscientious and enjoyed playing. Everyone could be, and at times was, a soloist. They liked the area and some bought Club cottages or lived in nearby Wilmington, N.Y.

One of the few delicate situations the Sinfonietta had to handle was the Club people who thought they could play as soloists with the orchestra. Against some, the Sinfonietta prevailed.

Now there are not many little orchestras. Chamber orchestras are twice the size of the Sinfonietta.

Dorothy Happel, violinist and concert master of the current Sinfonietta, came to the Club from Eastman in 1948. Most of the Sinfonietta musicians were faculty from the Eastman School and the Rochester Philharmonic. Paul White told the musicians they were "stauf" not staff (a different pronunciation to show more important rank) and therefore could come in the front door of the Club, be in the lobby and eat in the Dining Room for the reduced price of $2.50 for dinner. Dorothy was paid $55 a week and rented a room for $15 a week. Dorothy met her husband in 1950 and they married in 1951. They were entitled to rent a Club cottage for a reduced rate because of her status as musician and her husband's status as a New York University professor.

According to Happel, at first there were just two "girls" in the group, Dorothy and Paulina White, Paul White's daughter; then a female cellist joined. The women very carefully planned and coordinated the colors of the formal gowns they would wear. Day concerts were informal. Now there are more women and they just wear black, except in the summer.

Musicians' children could go to Club day camp. After the Club stopped grouping children as Elves and Pixies, about 1956, and for the next 12 or 13 years, Annette Albright, wife of bassist Philip Albright, ran the day camp for 3-to-5 year olds from 9:30

a.m. to noon when the children were picked up by their parents or nannies. The day camp was located in the bottom of the playhouse. Children, under Mrs. Albright's direction listened to stories and sang songs, played in the sand area, went for nature walks and to the weekly children's concert. Fun trips were to the children's library in the Clubhouse. Other activities included making cookies from Rice Krispies cereal.

Philip Albright played bass from 1948 to 1989 under both Paul White and Carl Eberl, who had taught at Queens College in New York City. At the Club he felt the musicians were treated well and the audiences were appreciative. In terms of being "treated well" Albright remembers Friday lunches of lobster for $1.25. As no money was exchanged in the dining room, Sinfonietta musicians paid the $1.25 at the Front Desk for lunch and $2.50 for dinner and could have anything off the menu to eat.

The Sinfonietta repertoire included opera excerpts, overtures, symphonies and Broadway musicals. When Albright first came to the Club, he sometimes practiced in Agora, which bothered the members so he was allowed to practice in a room by the golf house.

There was no exchange of members between the dance band and the Sinfonietta except for John Huwiler, a Yale graduate who came up with the band. It was Jeff Stoughton's Dance Band from Yale that played every night for dancing, and John played in piano and violin duets during the coffee hour after dinner. When Stoughton went to play for Guy Lombardo, Paul Jouard, also from Yale, took over the dance band. Even though the Club really discouraged it, they played Dixieland overtown in a place in back of the Post Office by the toboggan run. In 1969 John Huwiler joined the Sinfonietta and has played with them every summer since. Jan Elliott and John met at the Club. She was a waitress in 1952 from

Miami University in Ohio who thought the Club was a wonderful place that provided well for the employees, especially the dances once a week. This was another example of a couple, one being "stauf" and the other "staff"!

While the Sinfonietta was at the Club, it never had to worry about funding. The Club's CPA had affirmed that Lake Placid Club Educational Foundation money could cover 10 to 15 percent of Sinfonietta salaries as long as the Foundation had 10 to 15 percent control over renditions offered by the Sinfonietta. This would continue the tax exempt status. In 1965 a special collection from Club members was taken that netted $2,500 for support of the Sinfonietta

Due to the work of Dorothy Happel and Irvine Dearnley, the Sinfonietta incorporated when the Club closed. It now has a board of directors and raising funds is a major concern.

October 1922 Club Notes anounced that for 28 years the Club had been trying to have Village of Lake Placid churches meet the Club's spiritual needs. There was transportation arranged, including a ferry to the other side of Mirror Lake but it was admitted the churches could not do this unless the Club people would go to the churches. Since they wouldn't, a beautiful new chapel with Tiffany windows was built in the Club. An organ was situated in Agora Theater that could be heard in the chapel and was wired to the lobby and outdoors. This was an Austin organ, with four manuals including great, swell, pedal and echo. It had, to begin with, 50 stops and 3,000 pipes. This number increased (at least according to Club Notes) to 60 and then 80 stops in 1923. A $30,000 gift was received for the organ.

A chapel necessitated the presence of Club chaplains, who, accompanied by their wives, "appreciated the privileges" of a restful vacation. They would preach on Sundays and hold weekday morning prayers.

In 1926, the Acousticon [a listening devise] was installed that carried the service in the chapel to the organist (then Wallace Van-Lier), who could synchronize his playing with the service without depending on signals. In the 1980s Virginia Gilmore, organist at St. Eustace Episcopal Church in Lake Placid and Village Treasurer, played for two weddings at the Club chapel. For these (which were the last weddings at the Chapel), the Acousticon was long gone and Gilmore was provided with a runner to tell her what was going on in the wedding.

Gilmore took violin and piano lessons from Carl Lamson who was primarily known as the accompanist for violinist Fritz Kreisler. When Gilmore was going to Potsdam to play in a violin competion, her piano accompanist couldn't go. Carl Lamson went with her to accompany her. Gilmore is sure the judges were just listening to him because they asked her, "Is that really Carl Lamson?"

Carl Lamson was also the pianist and organist at the Club for years. For the summer of 1941, he and his wife were given a cottage rent free on June 12th. When Lamson was engaged as a member of the concert ensemble from June 12 to July 12, according to his contract, he was paid $40 a week. When he was pianist for the ensemble and choir director and organist for daily chapel services from July 12 to Sept. 7, he received $85 a week.

After Sept. 8, he would receive $40 a week as choir director and daily organist. However, in an in-house memo not to be seen by Lamson, Mr. Packer, Club manager at the time requested that nothing be said to Lamson about continuance of employment after Sept. 7 and that Lamson ask a less expensive member of the dance orchestra who also played the organ to be organist after that date. Should that fail, Mrs. Dwight Feek of Ausable Forks could be re-engaged as organist at her usual compensation of $6 a trip for either daily chapel or Sunday service; or both.

A contract was found in the archives that stated that beginning on Oct. 10, 1943, Frederick Biehler, a member of the Northwood faculty, would be employed as organist at the Club chapel for Northwood boys and the Song Service for the periods of three school terms and organist for any extra events during the same period. He also agreed to play organ and piano during the holiday periods when the school was not in session. During Easter vacation, if Northwood chapel was not held, the Song Service would be omitted. In return, the Lake Placid Club would pay Northwood School $200. Mr. Biehler was needed at Christmas for the following:

Dec. 24
- Wassail Ceremony at 8:30 p.m.
- Singing of Waits at 11 p.m. (waitresses and waiters)

Dec. 25
- Chapel Service at 11 a.m.
- Christmas Tree at 4 p.m.

Dec. 26
- Sunday Service at 11 a.m.
- Christmas Tree (employees) 4:30 p.m.
- Song Service at 8:15 p.m.

Dec. 31
- Father Time Ceremony at 11:45 p.m.
- Possible singing of college Songs

Jan. 2
- Chapel Service at 11 a.m.
- Song Service at 8:15 p.m.

One or two extra occasions may have been required, such as rehearsals for carols. For these Christmas accompaniments, Mr. Bieler was paid $5 per visit, or $50. If his services were needed at extra events at Easter, it would also be at the $5 per visit rate.

At a later time, Paul Jouard, leader of the Dance Band, played the organ for Christmas festivities that started with the finding of the Yule log. Howard Baker, Master of Merry Disport, dressed in costume, on the afternoon of Christmas Eve and took 200 or so children out to hunt for the Yule log. It had been prepared by Club carpenters, six-feet long with no bark on it and notched on one end so a rope could be attached. (It was hard to hide the log when there was no snow at Christmas.) The first child to find the log in the woods got the first ride on the log back to the Club.

The log (or a substitute) was put in the fireplace to the left of the stage in Agora. Two floor-standing candelabra were lit by the staff in the evening as was the Yule log to herald the beginning of the Burning Yule Log ceremony. There was wassail to drink and green boughs to throw on the fire.

At New Year's Eve there was the ceremony of ringing out the old year, a farewell to Father Time and a welcome to the New Year, played by a young child of a Club member. Everything ran precisely by Greenwich Mean Time. A large three-foot chrome pipe (a musical chime) was suspended by a leather thong from a wooden frame. As the last lines of "Silent Night" were played by Paul Jouard on the organ, an employee was to hit the chime 12 times with a leather mallet. Father Time would be on stage warming his hands over a fake wood fire. The New Year's baby would be on the balcony over the fireplace in Agora.

A Club story relates that one particular New Year's the chosen employee had been to a cocktail party at which there were two punch bowls - one filled with martinis, the other with Manhattans. This employee had had a few of each. He came back to the Club at 7 p.m. to take tickets for the kids' movie in Agora that let out at 10:30 p.m. He got through that without a problem.

He then decided to take a nap and fell sound asleep in the back pew of the chapel (right off Agora). At five minutes to midnight, he woke up and went on stage with Godfrey Dewey, son of Club founder Melvil Dewey. The last notes of "Silent Night" were played. He lifted the leather mallet, swung at the chime and missed. He hit it again squarely. Counting his first missed swing as one, he hit the chime 11 more times and walked off stage. The assembled crowd of 1,000 was left waiting for the 12th gong. He went back into the Chapel and fell asleep.

The next morning this employee was handing out hymnals and a member, Mrs. Keys asked him, "...if they ever got that man out of the Chapel last night?" The Chapel was near one of the bedrooms. Her daughter heard the snoring, raised the curtain that awakened him, allowing him to get out before the Security staff came, and to get to where the girl he had stood up was waiting.

During the Roaring Twenties, the Age of Jazz, the Club (as expressed in Club Notes) felt jazz was "a device of the devil for the feeble-minded." They noted Syracuse and Rochester police had been ordered to stop any dance where merrymakers dance "with anything but their feet." The Club felt the world was waking up to the propriety of the Club council's firm resolution in the summer of 1920 when 30 leading members agreed unanimously that it should have no more jazz music or vulgar dancing. This resolution was rigidly upheld in selecting a summer dance band for 1921. Club Notes of May 1921 stated that "jazz would run its course and only the 'socially green' and depraved would still like it. We shall have all the life and brightness possible without descending to the cheap, vulgar, barbaric discords that give grave offense to every cultivated ear."

There is strong evidence that the dance band played good jazz for the employees at Lakeside and overtown.

A-Blossom with Flowers

As the seasons changed so, too, did the fresh flowers that decorated the Club public and private rooms. In the 1930s George Beauregard became greenhouse superintendent, had five greenhouses, worked on the grounds, worked with flowers and cared for a five-acre garden. He grew a lot of mums and pompoms that he put in white five-inch pots with saucers to go on each table in the Dining Room. He made big arrangements for the lounges and for delivery to guests' rooms.

In the summer Beauregard had two female employees to arrange flowers. The groundsmen he supervised would help the women cut flowers in the morning while the grass was still too wet for the men to mow.

The Club had lilies at Easter and piles of poinsettias at Christmas, just red ones and white ones, not the marbled colors of today. Beauregard made wreaths with big red bows for the Club out of princess pine and pine ropes for over the doors. Deo Colburn had a big moosehead on the wall in the Club and, at Christmas, the moose got a big wreath with pine cones on it. Many pictures were taken of that. A 10-to-15-foot Christmas tree would be brought into Agora and decorated. Adding to these festivities, department heads like Beauregard received a $100 Christmas present from the Club.

Daffodil bulbs would be planted in hot beds. When they showed color, they would be potted up and brought inside to the Bird Room (which in 1918 was home to 14 canaries) for guests to enjoy in late February and early spring.

Beauregard's staff did porch flower boxes for the cottages. Just before the first freeze, they brought the boxes in and took 300 to 500 cuttings for the next year's boxes.

For fertilizer he used lots of cow manure and 5-10-5 fertilizer. He was always trying some new fertilizers to get better flowers. "Growing flowers is not hard work. It is time consuming and flowers have got to have care," Beauregard said.

When told "You can't grow roses in Lake Placid", he took it as a challenge. He planted roses, covered them in the winter, and the roses grew for three years until there was a really hard winter, but Beauregard had met the challenge!

He loved working at the Club and did so for 22 years. Club comptroller Deo Colburn was a good friend of his. If Colburn killed a moose or deer, he would give Beauregard some of the meat. They were good buddies but Beauregard went to Colburn and said he would have to leave the Club.

"If you want more money, I'll get it for you," Colburn said.

Beauregard told him by working for the Club, which paid Social Security but had no retirement plan, he had lost 22 years toward retirement. He couldn't continue to do that.

Beauregard was good friends with the supervisor of the Town of North Elba, who said he could do something for him but he would have to change his politics. North Elba was Republican and Beauregard was a Democrat. He became a Republican and worked awhile on the golf course. The superintendent of the Arena told him if he came to work at the 1932 Olympic Arena, he could make good money, earn lots of overtime and have a good retirement plan. Beauregard did "bull work" (which was everything) at the Arena. He was handy with tools, he ran spotlights, prepared the Arena for ice skating shows, and cut trees for decorations for the ice shows. Dick Button (the Olympic figure skating champion in 1948 and

1952) would come to skate at the Arena and always ask, "Where's Little George?" He prepared the Arena for Sonja Henie (the Olympic figure skating champion in 1928,1932 and 1936). He worked for the arena for 20 more years and retired with a good pension. He was married to his first wife for 62 years and to his second wife for 12 1/2 years. He lived in the house next door to Town Hall and his yard was a-blossom with flowers all season long. At first his rent was $50 a month, and at that time bread was 10 cents a loaf. He said he felt strongly that we are not making more money nowadays, we are just handling more money.

"Live and let live and work together," Beauregard was told long ago. "In those days, people helped each other. That's how we got by. If you were sick, all your neighbors were there to help you."

George Beauregard was 96 years old when interviewed on Aug.16, 2001 at Uihlein Mercy Center, Lake Placid, N.Y. and died on Oct. 21 of that year.

CHAPTER 4

Canvas Boots, Wet Sand and a Bounding Roller

Tomato cans; that's what started golf at Lake Placid. Joseph L. Harrison, librarian in 1932 at the Forbes Library in Northampton, Mass., met Melvil Dewey in the late 1880s and reported that golf at the Lake Placid Club had a modest start.

In 1895 or 1896, golf clubs were ordered for the Club. When they arrived, no one knew the names of the clubs. Three putting greens were laid out with tomato cans as the holes. This first golf course was created by guests doing the work themselves. The Club provided the teams of horses, and stones were loaded onto the wagons by the men. The ladies lent encouragement and served lemonade.

Thus the first fairways were created, but for years a ball striking the ground would bound back as often as it went forward. Golf pro Wes Jones said in 2001, "These courses were built by horses and mules and men's hands. They're not graded: they're much more rustic; so you get some odd bounces."

Greenskeeping was initially done, not by men pushing mowers, but by teams of horses pulling mowers. Special canvas boots were worn by the horses so their horseshoes didn't cut into the greens.

By 1901, six years into the life of the Club, athletic instruction was given in golf, driving, riding, bicycling, sailing, rowing, canoeing, and swimming. Club Notes in 1908 boast of tennis courts, croquet, target practice, and Merrylegs the Shetland pony. For employees these activities meant setting up nets, hoops and mallets, straw targets, and putting a very small saddle on the pony.

In 1909, Seymour Dunn, a clubmaker and golf instructor, designed the Lower 18. He had control of the Golf House, golf school and pro shop. Dunn played the bagpipes, had a good medical library, was very handsome and flirted with women even when he was elderly, according to his daughter-in-law. He got along well with the wealthy but there is a letter from Melvil Dewey that said, "Mr. Dunn, Please stop your children from running through the library in their bathing suits." The Dunns had eight children.

But also, in 1909, Sunday was quiet, churchboats [boats to take members to church] were free. Neither golfmen nor caddies were on duty. There was no swimming at the Club lakefront and no applause at Sunday evening recitals.

Other information from Club Notes shows that in 1922 overseeing sports were F. C. Herbel, tennis; Dr. G. A. Cornell, swimming; Jack Corcoran, canoeing; Fred Fortune, riding; and Seymour Dunn was in charge of golf .

Women caddies? Yes! In the early 1920s Frances Silleck was a caddy on the nine-hole course and she was not alone. There were no wooden or plastic golf tees. There was a wooden box at each tee that held wet sand. Caddies would scoop up a handful of wet sand and place the golf ball on the small mound so guests could tee off. She was allowed to carry one bag and five clubs. She caddied for either men or women and earned 25 cents an hour the first year. The second year if she was good, she earned 30 cents an hour and the third year 35 cents an hour. The caddy master had the time sheets and figured how long she caddied.

Dr. Lillian K. P. Ferrar, said to be the first woman doctor in New York City, would ask for Silleck as a caddy. When Silleck herself played in a tournament, Ferrar would follow her to see how well she was doing.

Silleck went on to marry, became a member of the Club and won four golf championships. Her 1974 Championship Cup is at the Golf House today.

Ferrar died at the Club and remembered Silleck in her will. She left her a leather-bound copy of a book on golf courses written by Seymour Dunn. Silleck appreciated the beautiful book, and in thinking about who else would appreciate it, called the Golf Hall of Fame in Pinehurst, N. C. They said they did not have a copy so she donated the book to the Hall of Fame.

Mary Wallace caddied once, earned four dollars, and returned home exhausted. Her father said to her, "You know, Mary Elizabeth, you do not have to do that." And she never did again. She spent her four dollars on a pair of huarches from Mexico.

The Club was just beginning to use the Lower Course when Roscoe Bowhall caddied in the summer of 1924. At first he slept in a tent and then moved into the Caddy House. A good day was caddying three times and one dollar was good for 18 holes. He remembers waiting in the Caddy House for golfers and really hated to caddy for four old retired Navy people. "They were pernicious!" Bowhall ate some meals overtown but enjoyed the meals eaten in the dining room located under the kitchen. They were good and rich. He also appreciated being able to use the Club library that summer. Bowhall realized that second-year boys who knew the ropes were paid better but he only caddied one summer.

George Hatfield stayed at National House across from the train station in the late 1920s and remembers running up the hill to the Club and inhaling the wonderful aroma coming from the bakery. He caddied for three years while Bill Dowling was caddy master. He worked all four courses and caddied for Albie Boothe, Yale football player, and Sonya Henie, Olympic figure skater.

By 1925, 200 caddies were paid by fees from players.

In 1937-38 when Robert Blanchard was 12 year old and spending time with friends in a store across from Lake Placid High School, a man he'd seen before asked, "Do you boys want to make some money?"

"We said, 'Doing what?'" Blanchard recalled, "because we probably wanted to go swimming."

"The man said, 'We don't have any caddies at the Club,' "so we piled in his car and went up there." It was the first employment Blanchard ever had.

The Club graded caddies A, B or C. Many caddies came in the summer from New York City and stayed at the Club. They got preference on jobs. The Club also gave preference to World War I veterans it hired as caddies. As a young kid, Blanchard and his friends were at the bottom of the totem pole. As caddies they primarily caddied the short course which paid 30 cents an hour for one bag and 35 cents for two. Dr. Flinner, head of the Northwood School, and Dr. Munro, Club physician, always hurried to make sure they got in within three hours because it would come to 90 cents, "and they'd give you a dollar," Blanchard said. On the short course, Blanchard caddied for renowned singer Kate Smith. After Labor Day the summer people were gone, the boys went back to school, but if you had good grades, you could get out of school to caddy when the Club had conventions.

"They don't call it Upper and Lower courses now but I always insist on saying Upper or Lower!" Blanchard said, proving he is an oldtimer.

In the 1940s Jim McKeen was sent by his family to live in Lake Placid with his aunt. It was common for 7 to 8-year-old boys to be sent North for fear of polio in other places.

There were 30 to 40 caddies consisting of town kids and the caddies who stayed at the Club. According to the townies, caddies residing at the Club seemed to get chosen to caddy first and were "away looping [going around the course] while we're here," said McKeen. Thus they became aviators, which was shortened to Aveys.

At 14 McKeen moved to the Mohawk building and caddied from 1943 until he went into the armed services in 1952. He said if he had not had the liberal education that the Club gave him in letting him meet people from other places with different expectations, he would not have gone to college. Caddying was a "shape-up" kind of job. If someone was a broken-down hockey player or a guy who lost his money gambling, caddying gave him a chance to pull his life together. It was an outdoor job that gave you the run of the golf course in the afternoon. A group of golfers was known as the Bearcats, so the little kids who caddied for them became the Bearcat Kids.

Mohawk, where caddies lived, was one of the larger lodges on the corner by Theanoguen, the Clubhouse whose Indian name means Whiteface Mountain. The food was great. The Club did a good job taking care of kids. They would get a box lunch that included two half pints of Lake Placid Dairy milk. Their laundry was done for them. They paid $6.30 a week for room and board. Club members paid a set fee for a round and tips were better than average for the 1940s.

McKeen said they were involved in gentler things then; like dances in the front room of the 1932 Olympic Arena and it was dancing together in your partner's arms. They also went to the Alpine Hut and the Birches. The caddy picnic at Mt. Whitney was a reward for caddies. It was a summer ritual to climb Cobble Mt. at least once.

All the caddies were very eager to have their photos taken with the Bauer sisters, who were young, blond professional golfers who held a golf exhibition at the Club. Caddies had access to guide boats and canoes at the Boat House.

Three caddies, Gus Miller, Ronnie Hames and Jim McKeen walked down to the carry [a path between lakes to carry a canoe from one lake to the other] between Mirror Lake and Lake Placid, decided to swim and took off all their clothes. A neighbor complained and "Fearless Fagan" of the Lake Placid Police picked up their clothes and took the clothes to the Police station.

At 17 or 18, McKeen got fired (or maybe just suspended) as a caddy because one night he woke up boys in Mohawk by turning the fire hose on them. Suspension was a better punishment than the beating he would have received from the college men. He did get to come back and caddy during Flaming Leaves, the season when the foliage is beautiful and it was hard to get caddies.

In 1944 - 45, when the Club was taken over by the Army, soldiers were restricted to using the Upper course while members exclusively used the Lower course.

Another caddy, Jerry Strack, was destined to become an entrepreneur because at the age of 10 he ran the Coca Cola concession at the ninth hole and was responsible for the stock as well as the money. He now owns properties in Lake Placid, and the Central Garage and Mobil station at the corner where you would turn up off Main St. to the Club. He has served in elected public office.

Sergei Lussi started caddying at age 11. He caddied for five years (graduating from high school in 1952.) He was a shag boy for golf pro Jim Searle. When Searle taught members how to drive, the shag boy down field would catch and pick up the balls as they were hit.

Lussi was so skinny his mother put towels under his T-shirt so the golf bag wouldn't hurt so much. He started off on the short course and as he got bigger, he caddied on the other course. He had a great time caddying and it was one of his nicest experiences.

He is now the owner of the Lake Placid Club Golf Courses where he was once a caddy.

"Al Durkee was a greenskeeper on the golf course," a Club waitress from Ohio, Norma Welter, wrote to the author of her experiences. "He and I became an 'item' . We didn't realize until after leaving how much of an item. It was not just a summer romance. We returned to our respective schools, Syracuse University, Syracuse, N. Y., for him and Miami University, Oxford, Ohio, for me. In February I visited Syracuse when we became engaged and we were married 6-14-47. We girls joked about connecting with a wealthy guest, but believe me, I got the prize! Almon James Durkee received a degree in architecture at Syracuse and came to Michigan to a distinguished career. He died this year 3-5-00. We had 52 years of memorable married life, 7 children, all a joy, and grandchildren, too. And it all began at the Lake Placid Club!"

From the time they were juniors in high school, four friends from Rochester came to Lake Placid to caddy. This would have been from 1957 to 1963 or 1964. Bobby Jones went to Dayton University and owns his own insurance operation in Dayton now. Mike Wolford is an attorney. Tom Niemtimp was vice president of several companies, just retired, and completing the foursome was Tom Mooney, president of Greater Rochester Metro Chamber of Commerce. They lived in the laundry building. "It was like being in a college dormitory, only we didn't have to go to school! We would be up early in the morning to caddy and then out on the course after 4 p.m. to play golf. We got to know the courses like the back of our hands. A lot of caddies came from Yonkers, Syracuse, Rochester, New York City and New Jersey. About 30 or 40 lived at the Club. Jim Searle was golf pro," Mooney said.

"All four of us were 16 years old, away from home and went to church. The priest said the church was in bad shape. The next

Friday afternoon 40 caddies showed up to clean up the church," he recalled.

Mooney is most proud of a photograph of the four caddies in their tuxedos on the Club's 18th green at Mooney's son's wedding.

Not all Club employees used the golf course for golf. Jack Kendrick (teacher, coach and playwright) ran the Lower 18 at sunset as a workout in preparation for the decatholon. His sports were rugby, boxing, wrestling, basketball and track. The Club also had squash courts that the employees would sneak in and use.

The position of golf pro was a significant job at the Club, not only for the golf instruction but as a major attraction to the Club, and a source of income and prestige. David Philo from Florida was hired for 1977 & 1978 by the Lake Placid Company to be the golf pro. According to his contract he received salary, furnished living quarters and linen service, and was required to maintain a six-month residence on Club grounds. Breakfast and lunch from the regular menu were provided for him and his wife. They could entertain members of their immediate family at staff meal charges. Room and board (staff meals and dining areas) were provided for one assistant.

The Company (Lake Placid Company as distinguished from the Lake Placid Club) provided Philo with a sales room, repair shop and golf club storage room free of charge. He had exclusive rights to display, sell, repair and service golf equipment and was entitled to all income from these operations. Philo had exclusive rights as golf instructor and all income derived from that instruction. He had exclusive rights to sell men's golf clothes and golfing accessories at the Golf House. He was granted permission to work out arrangements with the other concessionaire (Razook's) which had exclusive privilege on ladies sportswear, to handle ladies' wear in the Golf House.

Philo agreed to employ any assistant golf professionals as well as sales personnel. These persons were employees of Philo and he was responsible for their conduct and demeanor on Club premises.

He accepted the provisions of workmen's compensation and held the Company harmless, and indemnified it against any compensible loss. Philo provided fire, theft and damage insurance for all golf equipment stored under his care and control. Rates and prices charged members and guests were subject to prior approval of the Lake Placid Company and were reviewed annually. Philo's charge tickets for instruction and sales room operations were brought to the main office of the Company daily. The Company did not guarantee these charges but would make a reasonable effort to obtain payment for Philo's account.

He had exclusive rights to the driving range, provided he stocked the range with golf balls and assumed total employment of the caddy master. Philo was entitled to all income derived from the driving range.

His privileges in the Club were those of an executive department head. He was deemed an independent contractor and venturer while engaged as golf pro, with permission to seek employment after the season as a winter pro. The name Lake Placid Club was to be used as his home club should he enter tournaments.

Cal Lewis started working on the greens in 1971 under Rollie White, Superintendent of Course. He is greenskeeper today. Back then, each man was assigned six holes and walking greens mowers. They would mow the greens, change the cup location and use the whipping pole, then of bamboo, now of fiberglass, to break up the piles of grass. They would rake the sand bunkers and maintain the trim work that the mowers couldn't get. The grounds crew employed 13 to 15 people, same as today. Motorized mowers were available about 1955 but arrived at the Club in the 1960s.

On the greens they used milorganite fertilizer, which was human compost from Milwaukee, WI. They would go to train stations in Ausable, Westport or Willsboro to load their trucks from the train. This was done once a year in the fall. On the tees and greens herbicides are now used for weeds and insecticides for turf pests. Occasionally fungicide applications are used but the Club courses use 90 percent less than other courses around because the cool nights kill things off without help.

Irrigation of the Club courses was by garden hose and sprinklers at night. "Lots of hours at night! I can attest to that," Lewis exclaimed. "Wind is a problem in the winter because there can be six inches of snow but instead of melting into the ground, it blows off and the greens dry out."

The golf courses have kept going despite the Club's closing, except for one year. When Gleneagles was considering the property in the 1980s and there was the promise of two new Jack Nicholas courses, everything was let go. There was no cutting. When the promise fell through, Lewis and his crew had to use a Ford 3000 tractor flail mower and a bush hog to cut through the growth. The courses did open, however, in June of the following year in good shape.

Opening the courses to the public increased the number of rounds per year. On an average day in 2002, 300 to 350 people played the courses; on a good day 350 to 400.

Robert Reynolds met his wife, Beryl, at the Club when she was the desk clerk. When they were first married, they had an apartment and then moved into a furnished Club cottage right on Mirror Lake. They got room and board and free linens which helped with finances. There were great opportunities for children. The Reynoldses' two went to the Club day camp and skied. Reynolds was a member of the Professional Ski Instructors of America and Ski Area Operators of America. He worked at the Club from 1951 to 1980.

He was also a registered skeet referee, who in skeet tournaments judged if the target was hit or missed. The Club had five skeet fields and three trap fields. Skeet shooting is also called "clay pigeons." There are five stations in a semi-circle. There's a high house and a low house [shooting stations]. When the shooter is ready, he says, "Pull," and the clay pigeons fly up.The skeet tournaments at the Club were almost equal to the New York State Championships. People flew in from Florida to compete. Reynolds spoke of Fred Missildine, a well-known skeet shooter, writer and instructor who took part in these events. At the end of the shoot, there was a big dinner, and the Club always gave out nice trophies. Skeet fields were active from 1965 to 1975, one tournament in the spring and one in the fall.

Sports staff moved from activity to activity with the season. Zay Curtis, as a program assistant with recreational activities and the theater, worked with Bob Reynolds for three or four years in the summer. George Reynolds was a concessionaire who gave swimming lessons. Art Devlin would open up the beach in the spring and was lifeguard in the summer. He did no swimming instruction, as that would conflict with his amateur status as an Olympic ski jumper. When Devlin was a lifeguard, Sherman Billingsley [owner of the Stork Club in New York City] came down to the beach and pointed out his daughters to him and said to take good care of them. He slipped Devlin $100; and repeated this whenever he came. Billingsley told Devlin about the Stork Club and said, "If you're ever in New York City, come to the Stork Club." In December 1941 Art Devlin was in New York City with the Olympic ski jumping team. They had a couple of days to spend before they flew to St. Moritz.

They were looking around for something to do and Devlin had Billingsley's card in his pocket. He suggested they go to the Stork Club. He called for reservations and identified himself. The reservations clerk sort of laughed when Devlin used Billingsley's name but the reservations clerk came back to the phone immediately and said, "Yes, come!" The whole Olympic team went to the Stork Club, were well fed and given gifts; perfume for the women and cologne for the men. Billingsley certainly honored his Lake Placid Club connections. In 1956 Arthur Godfrey, who was best buddies with Billingsley, did his show from the Club and told the Devlin - Stork Club story on the air.

Devlin would take children mountain climbing. After he introduced them to water skiing, they wouldn't do anything else. Bill Hovey was running a little water-skiing school at that time on Lake Placid. Bob Reynolds would transport and drive the boat, and teach. They skied off the dock on Moose Island, which the Club owned, in Lake Placid, not Mirror Lake. They had an inboard Century and a Chris-Craft Penyan. This was checked out to teach the little kids. Basically it was behind the boat skiing on two skis, not a ski board as today. They did have slalom skis.

Winter activities included sleighing, saddle horses and a fine toboggan chute down the hill from the first tee were offered as early as 1906. Skiing at the Club actually started out as cross country. Ski John (Moorhead) took care of everyone's skis and waxed them daily according to the temperature.

There was a ski jump on the golf course. Dr. Hart related that Melvil Dewey heard his son, Godfrey, had gone off the ski jump on his sled. Godfrey was called to his father's office and confronted with, "Godfrey, I understand you went off that ski jump on a sled."

"Yes, Father," he replied.

"That was very foolish of you. You might have been killed. Why didn't you let Ski John do it first?" Dewey said.

That ski jump was dismantled and is now in the Village of Lake Placid park as the toboggan shoot that slides riders out onto Mirror Lake in the winter.

Staff in March 1908 "have built wind and snow breaks to protect from heavy snows which have buried our skating for sometime. This with our ice scrapers and engine and pump for flooding (the tennis courts) promise steady skating," Club Notes boasted.

Gordon R. Marshall was a skater who participated in the Annual Winter Carnival and in February 1919 set the world's record high jump backwards on ice skates at 3 feet 6 inches. This may be an unofficial record, as the day before the actual competition, his wife fell and gave premature birth to his first son, Donald, in the Annex. Marshall was unable to attend the official event. The *Lake Placid News* does state in the February 21, 1919, edition that "Gordon Marshall sprang an event upon the crowd not scheduled on the program when he did some masterly backward jumping at high speed. Gordon had done 3'4" on the Club rink. He did this and then after two efforts cleared the bar at 3'5", equalling the 'world' record, and will soon top that. Lake Placid is full of potential record makers." The actor Douglas Fairbanks, Sr. taught Marshall to somersault on skates by hitting off of a block of wood frozen in the ice and then landing in a snow bank. Again, the *Lake Placid News* stated, "Gordon Marshall, a Club employee, performed over barrels and into snowbanks (one of Douglas Fairbanks' wildest stunts) in a manner nothing less than heartstopping."

In 1942 Art Devlin was placed in charge of Intervale to supervise and get the 40- and 70-meter ski jumping hills in condition. Correspondence from Devlin from Syracuse University in October 1942 said he hoped to pass the armed services' aviation exam. He would arrive in Lake Placid at the end of the term at Syracuse in December 1942. Again, he was just named manager and was not an employee due to his amateur status. "I got lunch and that was it," Devlin said. Lake Placid High School boys were given permission to use Intervale since the 30-meter high school hill was not being conditioned in 1942. The Intervale ski jumping hill had to be well secured as it was a dangerous place for unskilled people. To be ready for use, the snow on the hill had to be kept packed constantly. This was done stepping sideways on skis, except when it was a really deep snow fall. Then they would pack with their boots first. Devlin had some local teenagers, including women, who helped him with this work. By March 1943 Devlin had been called into World War II and wrote to the Club as Pvt. Art Devlin.

According to Devlin, the smaller jump at Intervale now is the original 1932 jump made longer by placing a new take-off end on it for the 1980 Winter Olympics and using the same landing space. Art Devlin demonstrated his ski jumping expertise as a member of the U. S. Olympic team in 1940, 1948, 1952 and 1956. He held World Championship titles in 1950 and 1954, as well as numerous other tournament prizes.

At Mt. Whitney, the Club ski area, the T bar was installed in 1946. That was one of the reasons they hired Austrian Benno Rybizka. Bill Hovey was director of the Bruce Fenn Ski School at Mt. Whitney. There was the main slope and another half slope, and the way to the top was very narrow. "We had too many people at the top of the lift which created a big hazard as people were getting off everywhere. Every year we did a little more work to widen the upper slope, put in another T bar and trail, the Hovey trail. The 1960 T bar was poorly located," said Bob Reynolds, manager of Mt. Whitney. Cal Lewis, now greenskeeper, worked for Reynolds at Whitney.

In the beginning of the Mt. Whitney ski slope, the lodge had a pot-bellied stove and a table that could probably seat 12 people. There were two outhouses, one for the men and one for the ladies. Reynolds decided it was a little tough in the winter to get out there so they installed a kerosene stove in each outhouse. The main ski lodge soon wasn't big enough, so it was lengthened but that didn't suffice. A wing was then put on each end. The whole building was finally moved to the River Road skeet field in three pieces so a new ski lodge could be built in its place.

Tony Allwork was the architect for the new Ski Lodge, which was completed in 1962. Water was supplied by a spring and reservoir half way up the mountain. The grounds superintendent at that time used to drive out there in the summer to check on the progress. "One day we were driving out there and approached the lodge. The grounds superintendent said, 'Look at that! That's a $5 horse with a $100 saddle!'" He thought the new ski lodge was quite extravagant. The interior was all butternut wood. The fireplace took a long time to build because board members would come out and make changes to the plans. Downstairs there was rental equipment and they sold mittens and hats. Eleanor Majewski sold coffee at the food counter. She'd get out to the Ski Lodge early in the morning, make the coffee and make up her own hamburgers. The beverage manager was Jim Pymyer, and parties also turned extravagant with wines and the best bands.

Grooming the slope at first was done by Reynolds and the ski staff skiing up and sidestepping all day long. Then they got rollers. They would go up the T bar and ski down with the rollers behind them. "Every now and then the roller would bounce right over your head. Instead of being in front, we'd be behind the roller," Reynolds said. The roller was a three-to-four foot wide drum of wooden slats. Two Thyacol Sprite snowcats with four treads replaced the drums.

For Christmas and New Year's the Club had 24 or 25 instructors, as most people wanted private lessons. There were ski races at Mt. Whitney on Washington's Birthday with silver bowls presented to the winners by George Carroll, then Club manager.

Reynolds wanted to have snowmaking equipment (perhaps to counteract Dewey's statement about "Never have a good winter." See Chapter 9). In the early 1970s a well was driven at Mt. Whitney that could have supplied good water for snowmaking. Unfortunately, the board did not see the wisdom of snowmaking and decided night skiing, still dependent upon rather than overcoming the weather, would be much better. The lights were put in.

The main slope was the most challenging. Reynolds insists it is true he was on the slope teaching when it was 50 degrees below zero and a bright sunny day with no wind!

CHAPTER 5

Prime Rib Five Nights a Week

In the Kitchen

Prime rib on the menu five nights a week, lamb chops on Tuesdays, lobster Friday night, steak every Saturday, turkey on Sunday (but a light menu Sunday night) gave the Club a richly deserved reputation for good food. While members rested after a hard day's play and decided what to wear to dinner or which friends to invite, the organization of the kitchen staff assured that the dinner would meet and exceed members' and guests' expectations.

Jim Sileo was hired away from the Del Rey Country Club in Florida in the 1950s to become saucier (or second chef) of the Club. He had known then-Club Chef Ralph Burns when they both worked at the Saranac Inn. Sileo took over as executive chef when Burns left. When Sileo gave up wearing the tall white hat, black pants and kerchief to become food and beverage manager in a sports coat, he moved John Duffy to executive chef.

Food was received in the 1950s out by the General Store (over which waitresses lived) and wheeled into storage by the kitchen. In the late 1960s, a loading dock was built with big walk-in coolers and a freezer. The steward received the orders and checked on the quality of the meat before it was sent to the two full-time butchers to be turned into steaks and roasts. One of those meat cutters was Ray Donnellan, who started working at the Club in 1954 and was there for 20 years. The chef he started under was Paul Longo. Ray's job was to cut all the meat for the menu. Once every three weeks, he would receive whole sides of veal to be cut according to the menu prepared by the executive chef. He would receive 50 to 60 prime ribs at a time and spend four hours a day on the saw making them oven-ready. Today prime rib comes to hotel kitchens all "rub and ready". Once Donnellan "broke down a black bear" in the Club butcher shop for a man, and prepared some venison but none of it to be served at the Club.

Fish came by railroad out of Boston in wooden barrels with dry ice. Donnellan would filet the fish. Lobster came in live in wooden barrels. Other meats came from Tobin in Albany, N.Y.

Donellan prepared the chicken and ground the hamburg. He did no roasting; that was done up front in the kitchen. The Club kitchen was great to work in with lots of space, more space than the Hilton kitchen where Ray, at age 82, was still working in 2001.

The executive chef planned the menus a week ahead of time and gave them to the print shop so they could be formally printed. "Simpler speling", a Dewey invention maintained during Melvil Dewey's lifetime, meant guests would choose to order selections like "apl py, butred nu peas or stud pruns." The menus always had light items, such as salads, cold plates, and seafood salad. There was a hearty soup and a broth soup for lunch and dinner. In the summer, the saucier made cold soups - jellied tomato madrilene, gazpacho, consomme on the rocks (plain gelatin added to beef or chicken broth. Stir it once in a while. It would gel up and be served with a slice of lemon). Hearts of lettuce salad went well at the Club, but not in other local restaurants.

Members and guests ate in the dining room and the Adirondack Room, which had been converted in 1963-64 from the Tea Room. The Adirondack Room was always open for dinner and served lunch and dinner during the summer. Sidney Maxwell's mother was in charge of the Tea Room in the summers for the better part of two decades until the 1920s. In the 1940s Hazel "Skippy" Androski worked some evenings in the Tea Room and gained five pounds that summer eating ice cream. An old-fashioned ice cream parlor was in Agora, where Jack Kendrick worked at Christmas, making his own sundaes and enjoying maple walnut ice cream. The use of butter fat in ice cream was limited on Feb. 1, 1943 because of World War II restrictions. Before the cutback, the mix of the Lake Placid Club ice cream was 62 percent butterfat and 38 percent solids, like strawberries or other fruit. In comparison, the vanilla ice cream sold at Ben and Jerry's on Main Street, Lake Placid in 2002 was 20 percent total fat, Cherry Garcia, 19 percent, butter pecan 32 percent. The author was eating Aloha Macadamia - 26 percent - as she did this "serious" research.

The kitchen staff was peripatetic and thus there were also great buffets at the Golf House every Sunday. Ray Donnellan did an ice carving for each one. He would also decorate a whole salmon and present a whole turkey. The band would play at noon. In the 1940s Barbara Downes Strack helped serve lunch there from 11 a.m. to 2 p.m.

On Thursdays the kitchen staff would go down to the skeet field at 2 p.m. After members finished shooting skeet, lamb chops or chicken would be broiling on the charcoal fire.

In winter, at Mt. Whitney the kitchen staff would take 12-foot-long griddle irons and do pancakes outdoors for the skiers and serve maple sugar on snow. Hot chocolate and other warm drinks also were served. In the days of Al Woods as cook, it is rumored that the slapjack mixture was kept going from one year to the next!

Kitchen staff would cater to the cottages whenever the people had parties. Occasionally they would go to the home of W. Alton Jones on Lake Placid, cook on the grill and do lobster, clams, and corn.

During the offseason, Goodman Smythe, a Club cook, was talking with friends who were dreading roasting their Thanksgiving turkeys. Since the Club ovens would be on and the kitchen staff had to be there anyway, Smythe said, "Bring us your turkeys. We'll roast them for you." The staff had fun keeping track of Mrs. So and So's small turkey roasting beside the 24 to 27 pound Club turkeys. The kitchen also arranged for staff, families and friends to come to the cafeteria and enjoy a good Thanksgiving Day dinner.

The Christmas Holidays were challenges successfully met by the kitchen staff. Sileo tells that on Christmas Eve about 200 people were served dinner. On Dec. 26th, the house increased to 800-900. On New Year's Eve there would be more than 1,000 fed in the house plus the local members who ate in the Adirondack Room. New Year's Eve was a nice set menu of roast sirloin with mushroom wine sauce, twice baked potatoes,and asparagus with Hollandaise.

Ice carvings frequently graced the dining room, carved by Sileo or Donnellan. They did 10 or 12 different sculptures, such as a swan, bear, deer, elephant, and Scottie dog, which the guests would see once or twice during the summer.

The saucier made the Hollandaise sauce, pot roast gravies and all soups. The broiler cook did all the grilling and broiling especially on Saturday night - steak night. The roast cook specialized in the prime rib and also did leg of lamb, veal roasts, and baked chicken.

The vegetable cook had three assistants who peeled and chopped fresh vegetables that were put in the cooler ready to use - potatoes, carrots, onions, celery. The vegetable cook cooked the shrimp for cocktails.

Club Manager Truman Wright recommended that Harry Purchase, bellman, be accepted as a hotel management student at Cornell University. While there, Purchase had to do three summers of approved practice in a hotel. Since his first summer as a bellman at the Club was lucrative, he wanted to continue, but Cornell would not let him. Instead he had to work seven days a week, 6 a.m. until after dinner for $4 a day as a Vegetable Cook's helper. Fred Richards, a chef now at the Hilton in Lake Placid, was the other helper.

While the money wasn't good, the experience was. When Purchase later owned his own hotel (The Wawbeek in Tupper Lake), he had one chef and 12 or so helpers. The chef figured that he could get whatever he wanted from Purchase because if he quit, Purchase would be stuck. One day Purchase went out into the kitchen, saw some hash browns simmering on the stove, shook the fry pan, flipped the hash browns up in the air, caught them and the chef saw him do it. From that point on the chef knew he was not the boss of the hotel. Purchase could run the kitchen and cooperation improved. Purchase didn't tell his chef that that summer in the kitchen at the Club, a lot of hash browns had been flipped all over the floor, but Purchase had gotten the hang of it and it earned him the respect of an ornery chef years later.

Two fry cooks were busy primarily at breakfast and at lunch as some of the older members wanted omelets during the noon meal. For a chicken omelette, the cold meat man would send over diced chicken.

There was a bake shop with a pie man, bread man and pastry chef with their own pot washer.

The pantry lady had five or six people working with her to do juices and fruit for breakfast and fruit cups for dinner. They served all desserts as they were right next to the bake shop.

The kitchen steward took care of the dishwashing machines. Ten or twelve worked the dishwashers with two pot boys. There were runners who ran between the kitchen and the cafeteria downstairs.

Stewards helped with the cafeteria (called the Zoo) where the help ate. Bellhops, waiters, waitresses, caddies, activity staff, relish girls and bus boys lived at the Club or at home, overtown. If they didn't live at the Club, they could pay a dollar per meal and eat in the Zoo. It was a convenience for the Club, which wanted these people on duty and not in transit. According to Sileo, a couple worked together down in the cafeteria and fed about 200 people per meal. The man was someone who could make a meal out of very little or make a meal out of leftovers from upstairs. He would make hamburger macaroni casserole. When the dining room had beef stew, extra was made for downstairs. The vegetable cook always had extra vegetables.

And the staff always complained. The cafeteria was called "The Zoo" because of the treatment received, behavior shown or the fact that the eating area was demarked with chicken wire - explanations vary. In defense of the cafeteria, Sileo said there was all the milk you wanted, cold cereal all day, tea and coffee, fruit and puddings, cake, and yesterday's apple pie. "Your mother didn't throw it out, did she?" Sileo said. "The help complained like all they had was macaroni and cheese. There was always enough and always two dishes. It was just like when I was in the Army. We always complained and never went hungry."

Those who ate in the cooks' dining room ate better than in the cafeteria. For example, on steak night, the ends of the steaks were trimmed off for the dining room but saved and served in the cooks' dining room. There was a little fat running through the ends and they were a little tougher but good. About 14 or 15 cooks ate there, but not the cooks' helpers who were relegated to the cafeteria. Sileo had about 40 on the kitchen staff.In earlier days, there was a staff cafeteria on the first floor of Overlook and staff bedrooms in two floors upstairs.

Now then, back to that light Sunday night supper. It was anything but! It was a buffet with choices of seafood newberg, leg of lamb, omelettes, scrambled eggs, lox, roast veal, 1/2 lobster piped with mayonnaise, chicken, Welsh rarebit, pies and cakes.

The dessert of choice according to Sileo, however, was an Adirondack creation. Two griddles, each at least 20 inches in diameter, were set up. Pancake batter was ladled onto each griddle. The pancakes were flipped over with a big spatula (and the cook's hand to help it.) There was a big pot of soft butter by the griddles (always butter, never margarine). After the pancakes were flipped over, they were slathered with the soft butter and put on a cookie sheet, one on top of the other. A pizza wheel was used to cut the double pancake in pie shaped wedges. A wedge (10 inches long) was placed on a dinner plate, not a dessert plate. When the staff came in to do dinner, pure maple syrup was put to simmer on a stove to get more water out. When ready, it was put into the mixing bowl of the Hobart mixer to froth it. The syrup got lighter brown and thick and was kept warm beside the griddle. A big gob of warm whipped, pure Adirondack maple syrup was spread on and the Adirondack flapjack was piped with whipped cream. Sileo said, "They loved it!"

From Ray Donnellan's point of view, the Club kitchen was a nice place to work. The Club had class. It had silver service, which meant food was presented on silver platters and there was an array of table silver. Presentation was important. Donnellan said it was one of the greatest experiences in all his travels. He has worked at the Bellevue Biltmore in Clearwater, Fla.; Hollywood Beach Hotel, Montauk Point; Montauk Manor, Long Island, N.Y.; Oyster Harbor Club on Cape Cod, Saranac Inn and the Adirondack Inn, both in New York. Fred Richards worked at a hotel in St. Petersburg, Fl.; worked at the Club in 1948 for five years, spent two years at the

Greenbriar in West Virginia; was executive chef at the Mirror Lake Inn, Holiday Inn food and beverage director; and was executive chef at the Hilton, all in Lake Placid. For fourteen years, he owned his own restaurant, Frederick's. Fred and Ray, as they were written up in the Lake Placid News on Nov. 5, 1999, have more than 100 years of cooking experience between them, have been friends for quite some time, and their paths keep crossing.

In the Dining Room

Serving the food required another whole crew of workers. In the late 1930s, Cal Wilson was a busboy. He came out of the kitchen carrying two trays of milk. Someone had spilled grease on the floor, he fell and spilled the milk. He also refused to clean it up! The woman in charge of the college kids' dining room told him, "Don't worry. We'll get someone to clean it up." His busboy's job was to bring food out of the kitchen to the waitress stations, not to clean tables. He remembers his boss being, "a hell of a nice guy" and they would go out to have a drink together after work.

Mae Whitney was the supervisor of the dining room. Waitresses made sure they washed their hands before dinner because Mae checked. Then she'd turn the waitress around and if the bow on her apron was not very precise, the girl next to her had to cinch the bow. Audrey Thornton's impression was, "Mae was a real dragon but she certainly ran a good ship!"

At the end of World War II, Imogene Bryant was a waitress while the soldiers were at the Club. They went from the Club to Fort Dix where they were mustered out. She only waitressed a month because the pay was not good and soldiers were not allowed to tip.

For the summers of 1946 and 1947, Hazel "Skippy" Androski was a waitress. She waited on the Kieckhefer family in 1947, became a lifelong friend of May Lou Kieckhefer who told her, in 2000, that the stories from the Club were being gathered for this book. Androski and Carter Lockwood, who later married May Lou Kieckhefer, had much fun that summer playing silly tricks on each other.

Androski remembers afternoons spent at the Boat House, canoeing on Mirror Lake and crossing over to Lake Placid once in a while. Some of the waitresses formed the Copesetic Club and wore a kind of safety pin to show membership. Most waitresses were college students. Climbing Cobble Mt. was a favorite pastime. Jack Kendrick knows leftover steaks were taken up there for picnics. There was afternoon ice skating in the 1932 Olympic Arena in summer and places to go in town. In the 1960s Lisa Forest told of afternoons spent overtown at the Arena Grill, Freddie's or The Spot. She remembers waiters and waitresses lined up at the range in the kitchen to grab parsley before dinner to chew on because they felt it was pure chlorophyl to clean their breath!

Norma Welter Durkee had a friend at Miami University (her alma mater) who had worked as a waitress at the Club and said it was great. "So four of us from Miami applied, not expecting all four of us would be accepted, but bless Hudson Tanner, we all were and became dining room waitresses. None of us had any waitressing experience but were fast learners. One of the couples at my station owned a steamship line and I hoped to work for them and 'go abroad' the following summer, but love interfered. Life at the Lake Placid Club that summer was like a vacation 'college style'. It was life in a dorm with curfew, housemother and rules. There was a recreation building, all buildings very old, lots of character. Some of the boys lived above the fire barn and felt a bit safer than the rest of us from fire. All employees ate in the cafeteria under the Dining Room, chocolate bread pudding...yum!...I experienced watching first live lobster 'drops' into the boiling pot in the kitchen and was horrified at first. Standards were strict, our 'lady boss' ran a tight ship. I don't remember ever missing work. I won a controversy over dining room dress when I was allowed to wear ballet shoes (black flats). We often walked to town to shop and browse.... I kept my tips in a tennis ball can and filled it a few times over the summer. My parents needed the subsidy!" (Durkee letter, 11-1-2000)

Beverly Reid thought it was fun to be a Tea and Coffee girl. This was also Barbara Downs Strack's first "legal" job (she had babysat before). In 1948 Strack came to work at 3:30 p.m., set up the tea, slices of lemon, milk, cream, and sugar with sugar tongs. At 4 p.m. in the lobby the hostess poured and girls collected cups. Tea and Coffee girls had a break during dinner, ate their own dinners in the cafeteria and after dinner served demitasse in the lobby.

Doing rolls and relish was a preferred job as you were supposed to rove all over the dining room serving dinner rolls in the evening and sweet rolls in the morning. A drawback was the hot roll bin was lit with Sterno and could get pretty hot. When Cal Wilson served rolls in the late 1930s, there were hot bricks in the server which made it hot and heavy for him, too! Lisa Forest waited on one person who had a ritual about Sunday night popovers. She'd have to go to the bakery, get the popovers out of the oven and go directly to this person's table where he'd consume them within two minutes.

When Carol Bigelow Brown and Linda Blair were in junior high school in 1954, they were rolls and relish girls. For relishes, they carried trays holding four oblong containers with spoons. They held the tray and members served themselves. In the evening the containers held cottage cheese, watermelon rind pickles, olives, kumquats and chutney - the last two new to Linda. In the morning, however, the tray held three kinds of jam and one container of honey. Children took great delight in taking the honey spoon, dribbling it all over and putting the spoon back in so far that it would slide down into the honey. The look of glee of the child encountered the look of dismay on the rolls and relish girl's face! They couldn't reach into the honey and get the spoon out so it was another trip to the kitchen for out of sight retrieval and hand washing!

Blair thought she was being helpful to the waitress by scraping plates at the table and she was quickly told not to do that! Clean up was done where members couldn't see it. Similarly a waitress never handed a member a clean spoon. She placed the spoon on a small plate and presented it to the guest.

Waitresses were good to the rolls and relish girls. Privileges went with rank. A roll could not be taken by a rolls and relish girl but waitresses would wrap up sweet rolls and give them to the R & R girls. Blair and Brown thought the food in the cafeteria under the main dining room was pretty good - -better than home! Some members were better than others for tips. Oil people from Texas were particularly good!

The "Queen" of the dining room was Grace McBride who handed out the clean uniforms. She lived at the Club but had a poodle that she could not have at the Club. Every night she took scraps for the poodle which she boarded at Merrill's on Old Military Road.

Miss Casey was the dining room captain - a real stern general who made you toe the line. She wore her dyed black hair in a bun.

When Linda Blair was 14 or 15, she babysat for children at the Club. The children went to group activities. Then for 50 cents an hour, Linda read to them, got them washed up and took them to the kids' dining room. She choose whatever she wanted to eat off the children's menu. She would sit for two weeks for one family. Other Club staff members could come and visit her.

At first Blair and Brown lived at home and walked over to the Club. After they turned 16, they could stay in the dorm which was their first experience of being away from home at Christmas time.

They stayed in the old building on the 3rd floor. The stairs were rickety, there was a communal bathroom with showers and a long bedroom with 3 or 4 army cot beds and a sink.

Blair would go to movies at the Club and sit in the balcony. After work they would go to Freddie's which is now Mud Puddles or the Arena Grill where they could meet the Club caddies from "outside" (places far away from Lake Placid.) They also went to parties at the Boat House.

Harry Purchase taught Hotel Management at Paul Smith's. Because of his own training at Cornell, he felt it was important for students in Hotel Management to have hands-on hotel experience. He was not popular with the academic faculty when he pulled students out of class to work at the Club but he had the backing of the College President and it was to the students' educational benefit. His students worked conventions (General Motors, Lipton Tea, etc.) and were paid what professional employees were paid.

In the mid 1960s Lisa Forest was a Hofstra College student waiting table at the Club. She and 50 other college students lived in the Girl's Club which was a wooden structure and a scary place to live. A watchman went through the building regularly but it still felt like a firetrap.

The college girls weren't in tune with the traditions of the Club. They were assigned to wait on the same table all summer because a guest would stay for the whole summer. One waitress was taken aback when she first introduced herself to a particular guest, and the woman said, "Oh, you're my maid. You're my new maid for the summer."

If the college students didn't come to the job from a town (Village of Lake Placid) point of view, the Club was something they knew nothing about. They didn't know about the restrictions and had no appreciation for feeling as though they were supposed to be servants. College students thought the members were interestingly peculiar, rich and old (even though they may have been all of 35!) It was the 1960s and a transitional time for both the Club and society. No hippies were hired and the students were fairly well controlled or they wouldn't have lasted there, but it was a definite clash of old style values with the new.

The dining room overlooked the new swimming pool. Two parties in 1966 in Forest's section of the dining room who had exactly the same tables every summer demanded that their tables be changed so they wouldn't have to look at "this ugly monstrosity of a pool." Forest thinks they thought it was too gauche. Some people would know if their table had been moved a quarter of an inch from year to year and would move it back to where it was "supposed" to be.

Forest made a lot of money as a Club waitress. Room and board took most of the wages but tips, generally a dollar a person (except for people who were a little tight!) added up to $300 a week which in 1966 and 1967 was quite good. But all of her money went to Peck & Peck and other stores on Main St., Lake Placid!

In the early 1970s Debbie McLean saw waitressing at the Club as strict in the dining room but that could be put up with because of the fun in the kitchen. Each waitress had about 24 seatings. Big parties were easier because of the set menu so you just had to put tally marks as to how they wanted their prime rib done. There were five choices on the a la carte menu. One was Eggs Benedict and another prime rib. McLean checked off "medium" and "on toast" so the prime rib arrived on a piece of toast. The member lifted up the prime rib and said, "At least you got the toast right!"

Paul McMorris, Paul Smith's College, Class of 1978, had a car (a 1967 red Ford Ranch station wagon that he bought in Lake Placid for $90) and transported the "Pros from Dover" [hotel management students] from campus to the Club. The Friday evening shift went well. "We were eager and full of energy," he said. After the dishes were cleared, they'd usually head next door for P. J. O'Neil's for a few beers, a game of eight ball pool and, of course, "hunting for members of the female species." Before they knew it, it was 3 a.m. - time for all good waiters to be in their beds in preparation for the 7 a.m. breakfast shift. "On a number of occasions we enjoyed the comfort of our Club dorm beds so much, we missed breakfast entirely."

McMorris remembers a certain magic about working dinner shifts. "Glancing out the dining room windows, one could see ice skaters gliding by on the illuminated rink. And the clientele was generally well heeled and pleasant to the staff. I remember saying to myself, 'This would be a great place to stay.'

At Christmas 1950, Barbara Downes Strack decided she never wanted to be a waitress again! Miss Casey was head of waitresses and felt it was her job to grab the back of a waitress's hair to make sure she had a hairnet on and to pinch legs to make sure she had stockings on. The chefs made life miserable for new young waitresses who would get chewed out if they didn't pick up orders right away. If dishes were dropped, the entire kitchen staff looked askance! Strack wore a yellow uniform with a grey apron and headband. Uniforms were done at the laundry and had to be picked up on time. The uniform, headband and apron had to be turned in all together to get a clean set. Strack felt almost like she had to roll in the mud to get a clean apron.

Strack graduated from Business School, and worked four months in the purchasing department of the Club which was right by the creamery. She was brought a big dish of ice cream every afternoon but left the Club to work for a doctor and has been in the medical field ever since – where they don't check for hairnets!

After the 1980 Olympics, Paul Smith's ran a cooperative program under the direction of Harry Purchase involving the Hilton, Holiday Inn, Mirror Lake Inn and the Club. Students lived at the Club and for the 16-week semester rotated through various positions at these "practice" hotels and the Club. Students were assigned to front office, bar, housekeeping and kitchen. Part of Purchase's job supervising the Academics portion taught at the Club was to keep it in balance with the Commercial portion, which he did not supervise. If a student was a good bartender, it was the tendency of the Commercial supervisor to keep the student in that position and make a profit, while Purchase tried to move the good student bartender to learn another position. Students paid tuition to Paul Smith's for this experience and were not paid by the Club. Intervention was needed when students worked for free on a painting job for three weeks during this wind-down period at the Club!

This plan of having Hotel Management students spend time working in many departments of a hotel was picked up by Disney and Purchase supervised 15 to 25 Paul Smith's students in their practicum at Disney World in Orlando, Fla. for seven seasons. This is a good example of the far-reaching influence of the Lake Placid Club.

CHAPTER 6

"Restricted"

On an April day in 1910, Laura H. Lewis was on Lake Placid Club Road and in the Club to take the Thirteenth Census of the United States. Employees who lived at the Club were gathered, 39 of them including Mary Condalan, chambermaid; Henry van Hoevenburg, electrical engineer; Seymour Dunn, instructor at golf club; and Eke Cutler, teamster. The next name on the handwritten Census record is one George Furgerson, a porter. He is 21 years old. He speaks English. He is able to read and write. He emigrated from the West Indies to the United States in 1909. He is Black.

In the column headed "General Nature of...establishment in which the person works," the words "Country Club" were written after Furgerson's name as they were written for Condalan, van Hoevenburg, Dunn, Cutler and the others. For Mr. Furgerson, however, "Country Club" was partially erased and "Private School" penned in. Only conjecture can answer why the erasure occured but the possibility of a Black employee at the Club in 1910 was erased.

The Lake Placid Club Handbook for 1901 stated the Club has no "guests against whom there is any reasonable moral, social, race or physical objection."

Lake Placid Club Notes, March 1905 state,

> No one is admitted to full membership till he has spent a season at the Club as an associate or guest and knows that he sympathizes with its aims and methods. No one will be received as member or guest against whom there is any reasonable physical, moral or social objection or

> who would be unwelcome to even a small minority. This excludes absolutely all consumptives or others whose presence might endanger health or modify freedom or enjoyment.

By 1928, the Club restricted policy for membership and guests of the Club was refined to read, "It excludes rigorously every person against whom there is social, race, moral or physical objection. The race objection does not bar foreigners of refinement... from its founding the invariable rule is to admit no Hebrews... Except as servants, negros are not admitted. The fisical [physical] rule does not bar convalescents or even invalids who, because of themselves or their families, are otherwise desirable additions, except in cases where there is possible danjer [danger] to others or where disease is annoying or a strain on simpathy [sympathy]. No consumptiv [consumptive] is ever allowed to spend a night in a Club room." (Ackerman 39)

Club life, established as a retreat for teachers, librarians and clergy, grew to focus on one socio-economic class who would be able to afford to get away from earning a living for extended periods of time (or at least underwrite the wife and children doing so.)

While Lake Placid is way upstate and far from big cities, it wasn't and isn't made up of only one race or one religion. According to Mary MacKenzie, late Historian of the Village of Lake Placid and Town of North Elba, in the late 1840s Gerrit Smith was a well known abolitionist and philanthropist of Peterboro, N.Y.. He gave away many lots to free Negros of the State of New York as a humanitarian gesture. Much of this land was situated in the Adirondack Mountains, including the Town of North Elba, Essex County, in which the Village of Lake Placid is located. Lyman Epps,

Sr., a free Negro, was given 40 acres in North Elba by Smith and moved his family there in 1849. When Lyman Epps, Jr. died at age 95 on Nov. 19, 1942, his pallbearers at the Adirondack Community Church included Harry W. Hicks, Lake Placid Club secretary and Dr. Godfrey Dewey, Melvil's son. Blacks, though few, were in the area, some were landholders and some came to the area in the summer to work. In the village, one boarding house on McKinley Street several blocks from the train station in Lake Placid was open to the Black Pullman porters who overnighted in Lake Placid.

The Club refused membership to Blacks but accepted outstanding foreigners even though they were Black. While members and guests could not be Black, members themselves had servants who were Black. When a member's Black chauffeur drove the member and family to the Club, the Club accommodated the chauffeur with housing and meals at the Club. "The colored chauffeurs have a dining room at Lakeside with an outside entrance door near Winona so they don't pass through the building, while other chauffeurs have their dining rooms at the east end of Forest Hall." (Club Notes Sept. 1912) Chauffeurs, therefore were accommodated at the Club because of their connections to members and were separated from each other as well as from Club members, by race.

The Club focused on sports and therefore those physically adept, not those who were physically limited or handicapped.

The Club always had conventions of organizations the Deweys were interested in. In the 1950s when the Club realized that it needed the business of conventions to survive, Club brochures still stated, "Because of the nature of its operation - as an exclusive membership club - this invitation must necessarily be confined to a limited number of organizations."

The Club practiced paternalism in that it took care of its people and made decisions on behalf of its people that the people were capable of making.

Melvil Dewey endorsed a variation of Christianity which looked down on denominationalism ("the greatest scandal of our Christian church" (Aug. 24,1929) and preferred non-sectarian worship and community-wide non-denominational churches for efficiency and economical, not theological, reasons. His son Godfrey (1887-1977), however, is remembered in a plaque from his daughters Margaret Dewey and Katharin Dewey Martin in St. Eustace Episcopal Church, Lake Placid, as "Faithful Communicant, Vestryman, Lay Reader...". Their mother, Marjorie Kinne Dewey (1889-1970) is honored as "Sunday School Teacher, Choir Director, singer...".)

The Lake Placid Club Education Foundation sponsored the Northwood Schools which required chapel attendance in the Club Chapel. If a Catholic student wanted to go to Mass, he had to go to early Mass overtown and also attend the Club chapel service. "The result of this policy is to limit the enrollment of Catholic boys. The past year (1928-29) we had only one in both schools," wrote Dr. Flinner, Headmaster, Aug. 27, 1929.

The presence of those of the Jewish faith in the Tri-Lakes area is well documented by ownership of camps in Saranac Lake and ownership of at least one hotel in Lake Placid (The Marcy). The presence is negatively demonstrated by hotels such as the Stevens House in Lake Placid which included in one of its brochures,

> Notice. Owing to the protests of a large majority of our patrons, and the welfare of our business demanding it, we do not desire the patronage of the Jewish people. J.A. and G.A. Stevens.

The Whiteface Inn brochure after W.W.II simply stated, "Hebrews are not taken."

This, then, was the context into which 1,000 -plus employees from the local area were drawn each year from 1895 - 1977. Club members were accepting of these restrictions and according to policies had chosen to become members, in part, in support of these restrictions.

Employees were in a different situation in that their "benefit" derived from the restricted Club was not membership but employment. Hiring at the Club also followed these restrictions and employees hired were not Hebrew, not Black, not physically unacceptable and, definitely, not consumptive. Did the influence of membership restrictions stop there?

Children of Club employees were yearly invited to a Christmas party at the Club. In the early days, each child was given a gift of $2.00 which was deposited in the child's account at the Bank of Lake Placid. In order to take that money out of the bank, the employee family had to write to the Club explaining how the money was to be used. A pencil note to Mr. Colburn reads, "Please let Gerald LaHart draw full amount out of bank as he has to have his teeth fixed. Thank you, Mrs. Henry LaHart." To the Bank of Lake Placid, H. W. Hicks, Club secretary (co-signed by the Club treasurer) wrote on March 29, 1940, "We hereby consent to the withdrawal of the balance on passbook No. 11356 Gerald LaHart." Copies of similar letters are on file with requests from other parents. Money given to the children was still seen as the Club's money and top management parentally devoted time to governing the restricted use of that money

Master gardener George Beauregard worked for the Club for 22 years and resigned because those 22 years did not count toward a retirement plan. Employees were becoming aware of their own long term needs and the need to take action for themselves rather than depending upon the Club.

Melvil Dewey attempted to bring women into the then (1883) male career of librarian. His "Wellesley Half Dozen" had assisted him in greatly expanding Columbia University's holdings and hours of opening. He intended a school at Columbia to train librarians, had 20 women enrolled and then he was advised co-education had not been authorized. (Ackerman 11-13) When Dewey was looking for a Head Accountant at the Club, Dewey wrote, "It would look well, of course, if he had a CPA but that is a minor consideration. We would rather have a bright young man (or possibly woman) who could do our peculiar work right." Harry W. Hicks, Club Manager, in 1943, however, would write, "I may be driven into using a woman executive as my assistant, but I would prefer not." Was Melvil Dewey ahead of his time? The influence of Melvil Dewey championing the advancement of women was lost when the presence of Melvil Dewey was lost in 1931.

The Club arranged for the summer of 1946 with New York City's Trinity School for 40 boys; 20 ages 14 - 15 for caddy duty and 20 ages 16 -17 for dining room duty. The Lake Placid Company agreed to the proposal on the following basis, "1. Eligibility. Lake Placid Club's requirement of race and color must be met." These youthful employees met at least two of the restrictions of Club membership.

The Club banned the playing of jazz by Club musicians. Those same musicians, who on off hours played overtown, played jazz at the Club only for the employees. This breaking of a restriction would now be seen as "Advantage employees!"

One clergyman engaged in at least a 15-year long dispute on ethical and theological issues with Melvil Dewey and later Club presidents. The Rev. Sidney Thomas Ruck, Rector of Lake Placid's

St. Eustace Episcopal Church from 1916 to 1957, was tenacious, had a strong sense of his own and his church's authority and was outspoken. Tenacious, authoritarian and outspoken were attributes of Melvil Dewey, also. They battled over encouraging Club members to attend churches in Lake Placid rather than have the Club build a chapel. The Rev. Mr. Ruck was as zealous about his church as Dewey was about the Club. Dewey did have Harry Wade Hicks, Club secretary, to temper his written responses to Ruck!

The Chapel was built in 1923 because even with Club ferry service overtown, Club members preferred to stay in the Club and attend chapel at the 11 o'clock Sunday hour. Club employees living on or off grounds were encouraged to worship in a village church, not the Club chapel. Even within a Dewey sanctioned non-denominational chapel, restrictions banned employees.

Walking past the Club Post Office boxes in the lobby, you came to shops such as a yarn shop, Razook's for women's wearing apparel, Shehadi's for oriental rugs and linens, a gift shop, Mary Chess gifts, Ruthie's Run for clothing, the Club Pharmacy; all concessionaires who sold gifts, clothes, drug store items, and jewelry to Club members who strolled by. Concessionaires were carefully selected so that they fulfulled the buying needs of members and did not duplicate each other in the stock being sold. Terms were a 15% commission to the Club from each concessionaire's gross intake.

Correspondence to obtain a new jewelry shop for the Club started in March of 1941. This prime source correspondence is most illustrative of the ways in which the Club restrictions were applied to those who would serve Club members. Between $25,000 and $30,000 worth of modern and antique jewelry would be offered by Martin L. Ehrmann of Fifth Avenue, New York and Palm Beach, Florida. Darrah Cooper of Palm Beach, in the same shop at the Club, would offer modern, antique silver and Sheffield reproductions.

Deo Colburn, Controller and Treasurer of the Club, started "the normal investigation to determine the racial descent, methods of doing business, etc," (March 4, 1941.) In a letter to Ehrmann, Colburn wrote, "Mrs. Smith [who sought new merchants to rent Club space] has told us of your connections with the American Museum of Natural History and the Philadelphia Academy. We have taken the liberty of addressing inquires to them." (March 4, 1941)

The Lake Placid Co. letter to the Philadelphia Academy asked, "In that we are a purely private organization we need to check with unusual care the personal qualifications, the racial descent; and their methods and practices of doing business." (March 7, 1941) The Academy manager was out of town that day and the clerk responding to the letter did not know Martin Ehrmann.

The same request was made to the American Museum of Natural History, New York City. On March 10, 1941, Roy Chapman Andrews, Director of the Museum responded,

> In regard to Martin L. Ehrmann, I can only say that I know very little of him outside of the dealings which this Museum has had. Those have all been most satisfactory and Mr. Ehrmann has shown a real scientific interest in our collections.
>
> He has sold us some very rare stones and our dealings with him have always been on a friendly and cooperative basis."

Mrs. Avy B. Smith (Margaret) who had recommended Ehrmann and Cooper wrote on March 8, 1941,

> Mr. Ehrmann is not a Jew. I have known him for a long time and both he and Darrah Cooper are gentlemen and both very nice looking. They are not at all on the type of Shehadi [another concessioner] and are people that you and I would associate with. ...they are not chiselers and I am absolutely certain that there will be no difficulty between us or with you. ...I neglected to say above that Mr. Ehrmann is of German descent and Darrah Cooper Quaker descent. Very definitely Mr. Ehrmann is not a Jew and does not look like one. Mr. Cooper will be in the shop with his wife, and his name and not Mr. Ehrmann's will be on the window.

Similar information was repeated in a March 10, 1941 letter from Mrs. Smith to Mr. Samuel H. Packer, Vice President and General Manager of the Club. She added that the Roswell Millers (daughter and son-in-law of Andrew Carnegie) had given the Ehrmanns their home with all the servants in Miami Beach for the month of February.

> ...They know them [Ehrmanns] very well.

> ...The last person in the world that I would ever recommend would be a Jew so this letter of yours staggered me a bit. I know his connections are good but what ever your decision and Mr Colburn's should be, I feel sure will be the best.

From Palm Beach on March 11, 1941, Darrah Cooper wrote Mr. Samuel Packer,

> Mr. Ehrmann showed me the letter he received from you. There seems to be a little misunderstanding on your part about the management of the shop.
>
> I have a shop both here in Palm Beach and in Petoskey, Michigan. My stock consists of Old English silver, Sheffield and reproductions. Mr. Ehrmann will consign to me the antique and modern jewelry. As his firm does only wholesaling he will not be able to stay here throughout the season, but will come up occasionally and assist me. The shop, however, will be under my name and will be managed by my wife and me. I would like very much to know very soon if I am going to be with you this summer as I have to make arrangements for disposition of my shop in Petoskey. I will therefore appreciate an early reply so I can make my plans accordingly. Please advise me also how many showcases are available and what other equipment there is. P.S. I would also like to know the size of the display room.

Mr. Packer on March 14, 1941 responded that Mr. D. B. Colburn who handles the arrangements was absent from the Club, "immediately upon his return I will take up the jewelry concession with him and hope to give you some answer before the first of April."

On March 13, 1941 Mr. Packer had written to Mrs. Smith,

> I know Mrs. Smith that you would not intentionally recommend or suggest a Jewish concessionaire. However, in our cold blooded investigation the report came back that Mr. Ehrmann was of German Jewish descent; that he was not at the present Jewish but his ancestors were. This is confidential information Mrs. Smith and might possibly

> be in error. The only thing that it is good for is that we secure more definite confirmation about his ancestry and that is the reason for Mr. Colburn's thoroughness. I do not know of any Dr. Marvel [Mrs. Smith had suggested be contacted] in the Adirondacks, however, there may possibly be one and we will try to find him.

Mrs. Smith received Mr. Packer's letter of the 13th and responded on the 16th,

> ... was a great surprise to me. I still feel a little doubtful but always willing to be convinced. Mr. Ehrmann does not look at all Jewish and I asked both Mr. Smith and my aunt Mrs White what they thought. They both do not think he does either. Mr. Cooper told me a few days ago he had two brothers in the German army at the present time and I do not believe Hitler would have them there if they were Jews.

(Author's note: The United States would not be at war with Germany for nine more months, Dec. 7, 1941, Pearl Harbor Day.)

A telegram was sent March 17, 1941 from Darrah Cooper in Palm Beach that he had been given until March 22 to decide on Petoskey shop lease.

> WOULD LIKE TO COME TO LAKE PLACID BUT MUST HAVE SOME DEFINITE WORD BEFORE THAT TIME. FULLY UNDERSTAND CLUB RESTRICTIONS AM MEMBER OF EPISCOPAL CHURCH ENGLISH DESCENT

On March 18, 1941 Mr. Colburn responded to Mr Cooper's letter of March 11th,

It would appear that I started on the wrong foot and began an investigation of the talents and practices of Mr. Ehrmann rather than of you. Since it now seems that the proposal is that you and Mrs. Cooper operate the shop at the Club, and that Mr. Ehrmann will only come into the picture by way of consignment of jewelry, it is reasonable to presume that such a relation would only require the attendance of Mrs. Cooper and yourself.

Our method of operation is an old-fashioned and necessarily fussy one, consistent with our operation of a private club with a carefully restricted clientele. Would you mind giving me the names of some persons to whom I may refer for character and business references and who know your past method of operations. I hope they may include the name of the organization with which you were connected last year in Michigan, unless that enterprise was purely of a private nature.

At 11:30 a.m. on March 19, 1941 Colburn sent Cooper a telegram

DEFINITELY INTERESTED FOR SUMMER. CLUB EMPLOYEE WILL CALL ON YOU. CAN YOU HAVE BUSINESS REFERENCES WIRED HERE FROM MICHIGAN.

Also at 11:30 a.m. on March 19,1941 Deo Colburn wired William G. Dowling (Club caddy master) in West Palm Beach,

PLEASE LOOK AT DARRAH COOPER JEWELRY SHOP PALM BEACH AND WIRE NIGHT LETTER IF YOU THINK GOODS AND PERSONNEL APPROPRI-

> ATE FOR CLUB IN SUMMER. HAVE WIRED HIM YOU WILL CALL.

On the same day, Colburn wrote The Philadelphia Museum and School of Industrial Arts in Philadelphia inquiring about the "racial descent" of Martin Ehrmann. (This after admitting Ehrmann was not the subject of the investigation.)

On March 20, 1941 Colburn reported to Mrs. Smith,

> We seem to be making a little headway with Mr. Darrah Cooper even though it seems that we got off on the wrong foot in our investigation of Mr. Ehrmann.
>
> From another source I have the information "We could not get anyone to make a positive statement as to his nationality, but he has always lived in apartment houses which are and have been tennanted 99% by Hebrews of the better class."...How much German and how much Jewish they didn't attempt to determine.
>
> ...While I didn't investigate Cooper I should judge from what everyone says that he was free from all the suspicions which caused us to hesitate in respect to Mr. Ehrmann.

William Dowling wired from West Palm Beach March 19, 1941,

> DARRAH COOPER WIFE AND GOODS APPROPRIATE FOR CLUB COOPER HANDLES ONLY SILVER. EXCELLENT QUALITY NO JEWELRY LOCATION WORTH AVE. COOPER CLAIMS TO DO BUSINESS WITH YOU HE MUST HEAR FROM YOU WITHIN FOUR DAYS DUE TO LEASE IN MICHIGAN.

Darrah Cooper responded on March 19, 1941, to Colburn's wire that he didn't understand what business references Colburn wanted. Cooper gave the name and winter address of the owner of the building he rented from and could give Colburn names of his customers, "but it would be better for you to get business information from Dunn and Bradstreet."

First State Bank of Petoskey wired the Club on March 20, 1941

> DARRAH COOPER... HAS MAINTAINED ACCOUNT WITH US SEVERAL YEARS. SATISFACTORY BUT SMALL BALANCES. NO CREDIT HAS EVER BEEN REQUESTED. GOOD MORAL CHARACTER AND OPERATES A GOOD SHOP. WELL REGARDED HERE.

The Philadelphia Museum School of Industrial Art wrote Colburn on March 21, 1941 "...we can find no record of Mr. Ehrmann in any of our files."

By telegram on March 22, 1941 Colburn wired Cooper,

> OFFER CONCESSION ON BASIS OF CORRESPONDENCE.

A letter from Mrs.Smith to Colburn was sent March 24, 1941.

> ...If Mr. Ehrmann is Jewish I will be the most amazed person in the world. However as the world seems to be "cock eyed" at the present time one apparently can never be sure of anything. He does not look as Jewish as the Colvin's and certainly much higher class than some of other concessionaires such as Shehadi and Razook....I do know that Darrah Cooper will be in the shop all the time and

> can sell the jewelry as well as Ehrmann so if you are doubtful why do you not keep Ehrmann in the background.... being in a Jewish apartment house in N.Y. is no sign as Mr Smith's [her husband's] sister lives on Fifth Ave. and last fall told us that she contemplated moving because it was 75 percent Jews now. After she looked around found unless she paid much more rent than she was now paying she was up against the same thing. Mr. Cooper told me Mr Ehrmann was a Lutheran and had two brothers in the German army. However I am sure what ever you decide to do, will be for the best. Frankly I am so surprised my mind is a blank."

Hill's Reports, Inc. Guardian Mercantile Agency in a "STRICTLY CONFIDENTIAL" statement of April 3-6, 1941 New York Office wrote,

> Mr. Martin Ehrmann is described as being a young man of about 35 years of age, married, wife's name Rita, and having his wife and two sons dependent. He is native born American and said to be of German-Hebrew extraction. We could not get anyone to make a positive statement as to his nationality but he has always lived in apartment houses which are and have been tennanted 99 percent by Hebrews of the better class.

It goes on to specify their previous addresses where they "have always conducted themselves properly." The statement favorably describes his business and financial situation.

Mrs. Smith spoke to Darrah Cooper about Mr. Ehrmann's religion and Cooper said April 9, 1941,

> I am positive he is of Christian Lutheran faith... I had hoped for Mr. Ehrmann to come for a short time in August to help with the show of gems. Otherwise he will have no other connection with the shop. Would you kindly send me your contract or lease and information concerning the size of the shop and fixtures.

On April 12, 1941 Colburn wrote the Museum of Natural History, N.Y. and Cranbrook School, Detroit, Michigan inquiring of Mr. Ehrmann's racial descent; methods and practices of doing business. Colburn wrote to Cooper also on the 12th, telling him that the Club's inquiries from impersonal sources as to the racial descent of Mr. Ehrmann "are at variance with your experience. We are so careful about racial descent of any guest or member of the Club that we need to be doubly careful about any concessionaire." Colburn would continue to make inquires and "hope that their experience may confirm your position rather than the one we have obtained from independent sources. Within a few days I will send you a proposed contract and a sketch of the shop showing size, etc."

The sketch was sent on April 14, 1941, the shop to be "located on the principal corridor of our main Clubhouse."

On April 15, 1941 Herbert P. Whitlock, Curator of Minerals and Gems at the American Museum of Natural History, N.Y. wrote,

> "I have had dealings with Mr. Martin L. Ehrmann for over ten years. I have always found him reliable, a man of his word and strictly upright in his business dealings. "I have never enquired into the matter of his "racial descent."

Cranbrook Academy of Art, Bloomfield Hills, Michigan as of April 18, 1941 had no information at all about Martin L. Ehrmann.

Colburn wrote Cooper June 2, 1941,

> "We are setting up our shop for the summer and write to inquire what changes, if any, you want in the shop... unless I hear to the contrary, we will simply clean it and set the fixtures where they were last year."

By hand Darrah Cooper replied on June 9, 1941, "I expect to be at the Lake Placid Club June 15th. I feel sure that the fixtures will be satisfactory as they are."

Thus through a three month long "cold blooded investigation" of the wrong man, the Club started a relationship of nearly 40 years with a new concessionaire. Only during the spring of 2002 from the window of the Darrah Cooper Jewelry shop on Main St., Lake Placid were the words indicating another location of the shop at the "Lake Placid Club", removed. In June of 2002, in the display window of Darrah Cooper, close to the Hilton, there was a small black pillow on which rested silver crosses. On the first shelf of the same window, also in silver, was a Star of David. His firm, even after his death, follows the good business practice of relating to and selling to all customers.

Back to the Rev. Mr. Ruck. As the rector of the only Episcopal Church in Lake Placid, he saw the Club as part of his parish. Following Canon 19 (exists today as Title 3, Canon 14, Sect 4a of the Episcopal Canons) which states Episcopal clergy need the permission of the resident rector before they can function as clergy in his parish, Ruck expected the Club to get his approval before it employed Episcopal clergy as Club chaplains. This was reluctantly granted by Melvil Dewey. The Club invited clergymen and their wives to stay at the Club for an honorarium if they would conduct services according to the Club order of service and preach sermons "of no more than 3 minutes."

As a clergyman, Mr. Ruck was given Associate Membership in the Club and he was accused by Melvil Dewey in 1928 of "boring in" – to take advantage of his Club membership to change the Club from within.

In 1936, after Melvil Dewey's death, Mr. Ruck requested that the Club cease being "restricted" and become open to the public. Samuel Packer, Club president responded, "...to generally open up the Club...I feel would be extremely unwise." (letter 12-21-36) (Correspondence from LPC Archives)

The isolated location was not the cause of the existence of the single race, one religion Club. Discrimination, legal within a private club, was the reason. The ethical nature of the practice is another issue. What is legal is not always what is ethical. The machinations of applying those restrictions to the concessionaire colored the Club policies and management. The pragmatism of the concessionaire and other employees who appreciated their employment colored their response. Discrimination of the kind practiced by the Club touched on many aspects of life and was not limited to its membership. Such discrimination weaves a wide, sticky web and entraps both the willing and the unsuspecting.

Lake Forest, Campbell rooms first floor above entrance sign

CAMPBELL PHOTO

Campbell arrival at LPC, luggage handled by bellman 1959

CAMPBELL PHOTO

Forest Lobby and Post Office entrance. Note icicles 1959

CAMPBELL PHOTO

Forest Front Desk decorated for Christmas LPC ARCHIVES

Forest Lobby Fireplace LPC ARCHIVES

Forest Clubhouse Lobby showing "overtown" across Mirror Lake through the French plate glass windows. LPC ARCHIVES

Forest Lobby corridor past the U.S. Post Office to Garth Lounge LPC ARCHIVES

In the Library. Painting of Harriet Hicks (Mrs. Harry W.) over fireplace LPC ARCHIVES

Site for conventions, dances and New Year's Eve celebrations.
CAMPBELL COLLECTION

Theanoguen the second Clubhouse LPC ARCHIVES

Theatre entrance by pillars, hotel-like rooms opened in 1924. Rooms with less character than Forest but safer. CAMPBELL COLLECTION

Club Chapel with Tiffany stained glass windows where short daily services were held, sermons limited to 3 minutes. CAMPBELL COLLECTION

One of the cottages, Outlook LPC ARCHIVES

Where milking machines were tried out. CAMPBELL COLLECTION.

Lake Placid Club

Melvil Dewey, Honorary president
Henry Evertson Cobb, President
William Scheerer, Vice-president
William Shillaber, Vice-president
Mrs F F Fletcher, Vice-president
Henry F Miller, Vice-president
Frederick T Kelsey, Vice-president
John W Hornor, Vice-president
Harry Wade Hicks, Secretary
Miss Sibylla Schilling, Asst secretary
T Edward Ross, Tresurer
O L Colburn, Asst tresurer

Lake Placid Club

In Adirondaks on lakes Placid, Mirror, Hart
Upper and Lower Cascade
Founded 1895 Open all year

Clubhouses
Forest Lakesyd Theanoguen
Northwood Kobl Mohawk Westwood
Cascade Adirondak Loj
100 residence houses

P O address: Lake Placid Club, N Y

Simpler spelling

Lake Placid Co

Operating Club Estate
Melvil Dewey, President
Godfrey Dewey, Vice-president
Emily Dewey, Vice-president
H W Hicks, Vice-president
C W Holt, Vice-pres & Secretary
Deo B Colburn, Vice-pres & Controler
J C Jubin, Tresurer
O L Colburn, Cashier

Lake Placid Club in Florida
on Lakes Placid and June-in-Winter
Lake Placid, Hylands co. Fla
Club Loj open Nov. 1 to May 1

Seymour Dunn, Golf Architect
Deo B Colburn, Golf Director

Golf director's offis

16 My 30

George W Hatfield
405 Seneca St
Oneida N Y

Dear Mr Hatfield:

We hav again reviewed your application and our grading of your work during previous years and ar willing to admit yu to our grounds where yu may offer your services as caddy to gests and members privileged to play on our golf courses.

Unless we hear from yu to the contrary, we wil expect yu 25 Je. It is essential that yu regard this date as definite and report accordingly, for with other caddys coming yu may be disappointed if yu come earlier or later.

On your arrival at Lake Placid, report to the Caddy Master at the Club showing him this notice as your identification. He wil hav information for yu about your living quarters.

Very truly,

D B Colburn

Golf Director

DBC/S

Letter of Employment for George Hatfield as caddy, 1930, note use of "simpler speling." HATFIELD COLLECTION

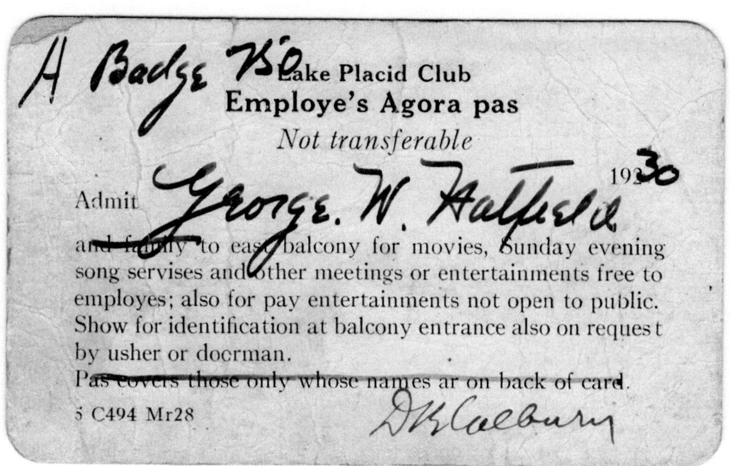

A Badge 750

Lake Placid Club
Employe's Agora pas
Not transferable

19 30

Admit George. W. Hatfield

and family to east balcony for movies, Sunday evening song servises and other meetings or entertainments free to employes; also for pay entertainments not open to public. Show for identification at balcony entrance also on request by usher or doorman.

Pas covers those only whose names ar on back of card.

5 C494 Mr28

D K Colbury

Employe's Agora pas, 1930 HATFIELD COLLECTION

Cobble Mountain, climbed once a summer by waiters, caddies, waitresses. 1930 HATFIELD COLLECTION

Room 749 in Forest Towers, 1962 LPC ARCHIVES

Room 809B in Agora LPC ARCHIVES

Forest East Suite in 1963 LPC ARCHIVES

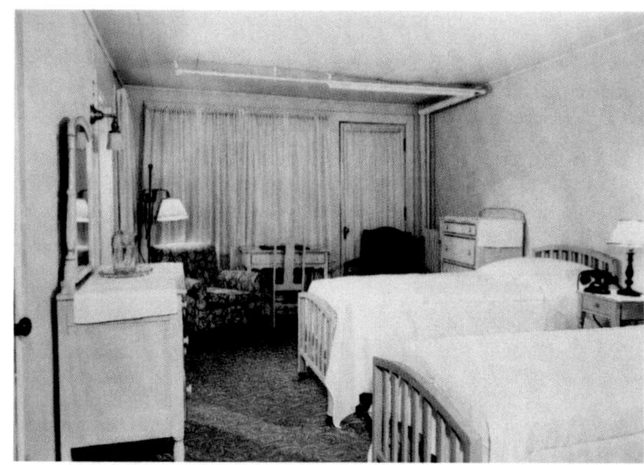

Room 599 in Lake Forest LPC ARCHIVES

First floor of one of the cottages, Edgewood LPC ARCHIVES

Bedroom of Edgewood cottage LPC ARCHIVES

Tailor LPC ARCHIVES

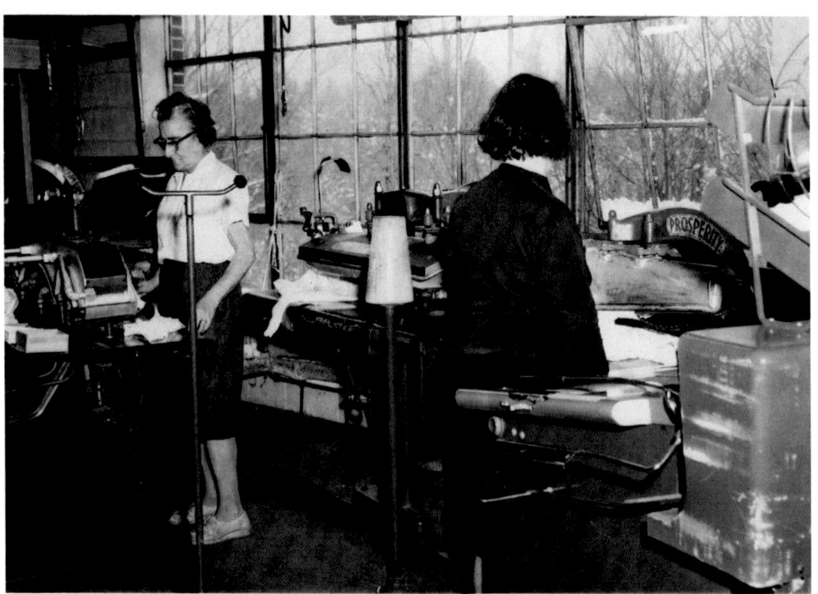

Presses in the Laundry. Anna Myers and Frances Hosler

LPC ARCHIVES

Some of the 22 tennis courts outside Agora LPC ARCHIVES

Skeet shooting off River Road, 1950 BAKER PHOTO

Sailboats at Boat House 1959 LPC ARCHIVES

Club beach on Mirror Lake in front of Club LPC ARCHIVES

Waterskiing on Lake Placid, Franny McKeown and Art Devlin BAKER PHOTO

Waterfront instructors and guard, foreground Frank Benham, dance instructor LPC ARCHIVES

Stone masons and hod carriers about 1900. George Marshall, far left with trowel and mortarboard. Ernie Hough 4th from left. PETERS PHOTO

Carpenter Shop and Mill early 1900s. Top row: George Marshall, Tally Preston, Dick Musgrove, 2nd row:-- ,--, Calvin Marshall,--, Art Squires PETERS PHOTO

Fire Drill. CAMPBELL COLLECTION

Lakeside Fire Equipment

BARRY COLLECTION IN LAKE PLACID, CENTER FOR THE ARTS

LPC postcard photo. Probably Melvil Dewey in white suit and hat standing left. Gordon Marshall, same row 5th from left circa 1915 PETERS PHOTO

Florence Marshall, pregnant with Don Marshall, winter 1918-1919. Karen Marshall Peters' Uncle Don was born in the Club Annex PETERS PHOTO

Flag lowering at Day Camp, 4th of July 1963 LPC ARCHIVES

Horseback lessons August 1963 LPC ARCHIVES

Kitchen Staff 1962-64, left with hat Arthur Dick, Garden Manager; Al Glass, Baker; Libby Cross, Pantry Lady; Jim Sileo, Executive Chef; Emma Franco, Head Pantry Lady (Desserts), Goodman Smythe, Purchasing Steward SILEO PHOTO

Shrove Tuesday flapjacks and race while flipping pancakes. Goodman Smythe at Mt. Whitney Ski Lodge LPC ARCHIVES

Lunch at Skeet Shoot 1963, Thursday and London Broil, right Goodman Smythe LPC ARCHIVES

Buffet table 1974. Ray Donellen, center rear. Note Club monogram on plates LPC ARCHIVES

4th of July Buffet at Golf House. In business suit Ben King, Maitr'd at Golf House, Eleanor Majewski, Jim Sileo, Executive Chef SILEO PHOTO

Jimmy and Marion Sileo still cooking hot dogs this time for the Library Book Fair 2001 CAMPBELL PHOTO

Adirondack Room Friday Night Buffet. John Duffy, Second Cook; Jim Sileo, Executive Chef; Goodman Smythe SILEO PHOTO

Part of the Dining Room 1966 LPC ARCHIVES

Christmas dessert buffet table, candlesticks of ice LPC ARCHIVES

Caddies 1930. George W. Hatfield, back row scratching his head HATFIELD COLLECTION

The Drovery where caddies were quartered 1930. "A noisy, fun place for a bunch of teenagers to spend the summer." HATFIELD COLLECTION

Inside the Caddery where caddies lived 1930 HATFIELD COLLECTION

One of the beautiful fairways at the Club. CAMPBELL COLLECTION

Grooming the Golf Course BARRY COLLECTION IN LAKE PLACID, CENTER FOR THE ARTS

Lake Placid Club
Caddy ticket

Engaged | Discharged

Amount due .... cents

.... Caddy

Tear off and give to caddy

Mark below quality of service rendered by caddy.

A Admirable C Common
B Good D Doubtful
E Eliminate

Caddy name ....
Deserves grade ....
Signed ....

Drop in box at Golfhouse

RULES

Caddies must:

1 Replace divots.
2 Be silent on courses.
3 Never walk in traps.
4 Never move while player is making shot.
5 Smooth over foot and club marks of players in traps.
6 Not stand in line of putts except when at flag.
7 Deliver to player all balls found on courses.

50 G340 My41

Would the Club continue to employ a "common" caddie? CAMPBELL COLLECTION

1950s caddies, Charles "Beaver" White, Sergei Lussi, Jim McKeen, Richard "Bud" Brownell, Craig Lussi. MCKEEN PHOTO

Admiring caddies around the Bauer sisters, professional golfers 1950-51 MCKEEN PHOTO

Backward high jump on skates discontinued because of the danger involved. PETERS PHOTO

Snow Cat on the slope LPC ARCHIVES

Mt. Whitney grooming equipment 1960s LPC ARCHIVES

Snow Plow lessons at Mt Whitney LPC ARCHIVES

THE TOBOGGAN SLIDE AT LAKE PLACID CLUB, LAKE PLACID, N. Y.

CAMPBELL COLLECTION

Daytime hockey on Mirror Lake, Whiteface Moutain, far left background. No parking problem here until the ice growls! 1919. PETERS PHOTO

Art Devlin in the air at 40 meter jump, 1959 BAKER PHOTO

Lower rope tow, Fred Richards, ski instructor, later Executive Chef, Lake Placid Hilton Hotel BAKER PHOTO

From the top of the T bar, Sergei Lussi, 1950 BAKER PHOTO

Marguerite and Gordon Campbell outside Forest on edge of ice skating rink February 1961 CAMPBELL PHOTO

The easy way to ice skate Marguerite Campbell seated, pushed by Barbara Campbell CAMPBELL PHOTO

Snow plowing the ice skating rink (frozen tennis courts) LPC ARCHIVES

Mt. Whitney Ski Lodge, Gordon and Barbara Campbell, February 1966 CAMPBELL PHOTO

Inside Mt Whitney Ski Lodge, band playing, night skiing outside, 1978 LPC ARCHIVES

Night skiing at Mt Whitney 1978 LPC ARCHIVES

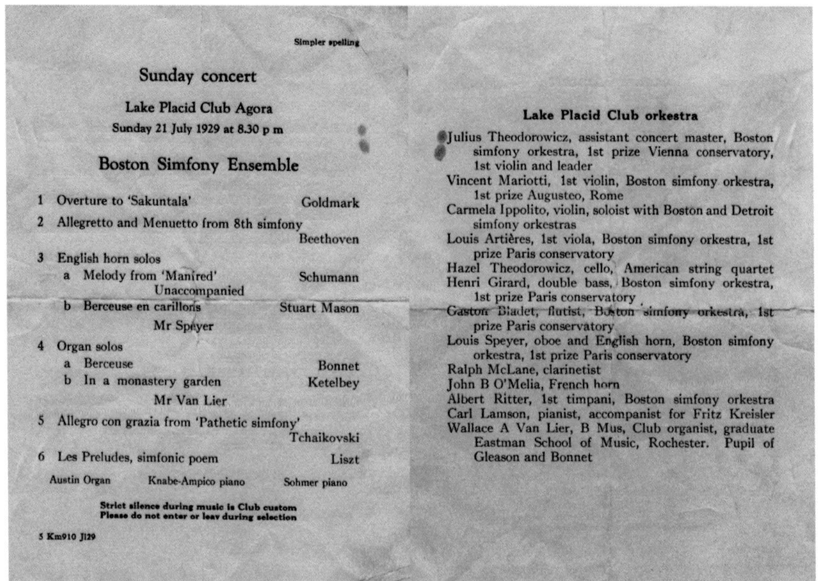

Simpler spelling

Sunday concert

Lake Placid Club Agora
Sunday 21 July 1929 at 8.30 p m

Boston Simfony Ensemble

1 Overture to 'Sakuntala' — Goldmark
2 Allegretto and Menuetto from 8th simfony — Beethoven
3 English horn solos
   a Melody from 'Manfred' — Schumann
      Unaccompanied
   b Berceuse en carillons — Stuart Mason
      Mr Speyer
4 Organ solos
   a Berceuse — Bonnet
   b In a monastery garden — Ketelbey
      Mr Van Lier
5 Allegro con grazia from 'Pathetic simfony' — Tchaikovski
6 Les Preludes, simfonic poem — Liszt

Austin Organ — Knabe-Ampico piano — Sohmer piano

Strict silence during music is Club custom
Please do not enter or leav during selection

5 Km910 Jl29

Lake Placid Club orkestra

Julius Theodorowicz, assistant concert master, Boston simfony orkestra, 1st prize Vienna conservatory, 1st violin and leader
Vincent Mariotti, 1st violin, Boston simfony orkestra, 1st prize Augusteo, Rome
Carmela Ippolito, violin, soloist with Boston and Detroit simfony orkestras
Louis Artières, 1st viola, Boston simfony orkestra, 1st prize Paris conservatory
Hazel Theodorowicz, cello, American string quartet
Henri Girard, double bass, Boston simfony orkestra, 1st prize Paris conservatory
Gaston Bladet, flutist, Boston simfony orkestra, 1st prize Paris conservatory
Louis Speyer, oboe and English horn, Boston simfony orkestra, 1st prize Paris conservatory
Ralph McLane, clarinetist
John B O'Melia, French horn
Albert Ritter, 1st timpani, Boston simfony orkestra
Carl Lamson, pianist, accompanist for Fritz Kreisler
Wallace A Van Lier, B Mus, Club organist, graduate Eastman School of Music, Rochester. Pupil of Gleason and Bonnet

Boston Simfony Ensemble, 1929, predated the Sinfonietta HATFIELD COLLECTION

Sinfonietta 1950. Dr. Paul White, conductor, Philip Albright, bass LPC ARCHIVES

Sinfonietta playing in the Music Room 1960s: Abram Boone, violin; Paul White, conductor; Dorothy Happel, violin; Paul Makara, violin; Sam Minasian, violin; Carl Eberl, viola; Ardyth Alton, cello; Don McDonald, flute; Carl Lamson, piano; Robert Sprinkle, oboe; Ross Powell, clarinet; David van Hoesin, bassoon; Milan Yancich, French horn; Charles Gleaves, trumpet. LPC ARCHIVES

Sinfonietta plays at the Golf House, 1976, Carl Eberl, conductor; Mark Yancich, percussion; David Greenhoe, trumpet; Don McDonald, flute; Sam Minasian, violin; Paul Wexler, clarinet; Dorothy Happel, violin; David van Hoesin, bassoon; Phil Albright, bass; Ann Aton, 1st cello; Gretchen van Hoesin, harp. LPC ARCHIVES

Howard Baker, right center, and the Gathering of the Yule Log. 1953 BAKER COLLECTION

C. H. Belknap of Malone repairing the organ console in Agora 1950 BAKER PHOTO

C. H. Belknap points out Agora organ pipes BAKER PHOTO

Organ pipes in Music Room during 1950 repairs BAKER PHOTO

Darrah Cooper jewelry shop in Forest. Note LPC design green and pinecone carpeting LPC ARCHIVES

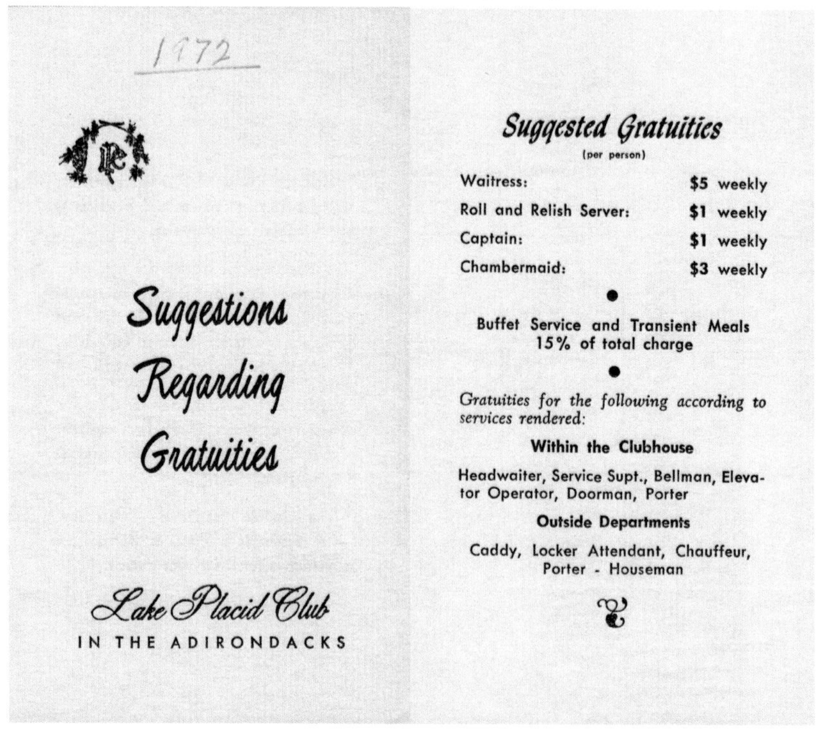

1972

Suggestions Regarding Gratuities

Lake Placid Club
IN THE ADIRONDACKS

Suggested Gratuities
(per person)

Waitress:	$5 weekly
Roll and Relish Server:	$1 weekly
Captain:	$1 weekly
Chambermaid:	$3 weekly

•

Buffet Service and Transient Meals
15% of total charge

•

Gratuities for the following according to services rendered:

Within the Clubhouse

Headwaiter, Service Supt., Bellman, Elevator Operator, Doorman, Porter

Outside Departments

Caddy, Locker Attendant, Chauffeur, Porter - Houseman

Waitress $5 per person per week = 21 meals and a $5 tip? Ah, the good old days! CAMPBELL COLLECTION

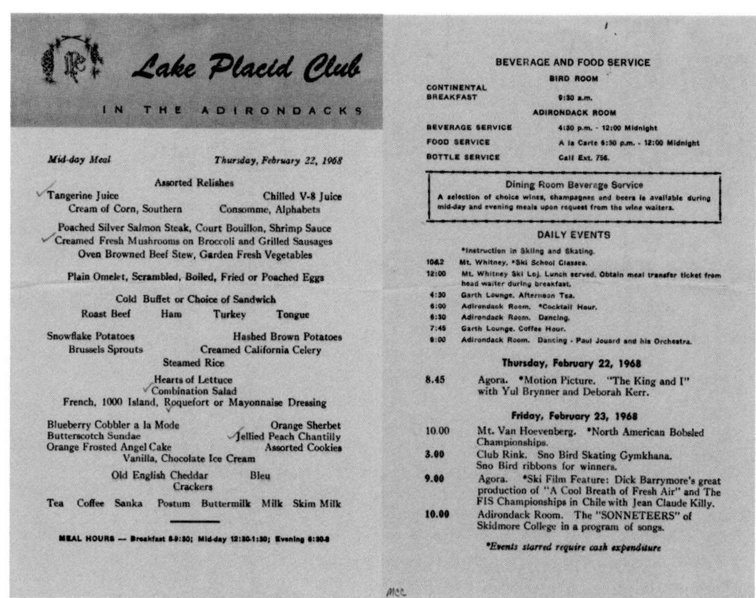

Lake Placid Club

IN THE ADIRONDACKS

Mid-day Meal *Thursday, February 22, 1968*

Assorted Relishes

Tangerine Juice — Chilled V-8 Juice

Cream of Corn, Southern — Consomme, Alphabets

Poached Silver Salmon Steak, Court Bouillon, Shrimp Sauce

Creamed Fresh Mushrooms on Broccoli and Grilled Sausages

Oven Browned Beef Stew, Garden Fresh Vegetables

Plain Omelet, Scrambled, Boiled, Fried or Poached Eggs

Cold Buffet or Choice of Sandwich

Roast Beef — Ham — Turkey — Tongue

Snowflake Potatoes — Hashed Brown Potatoes

Brussels Sprouts — Creamed California Celery

Steamed Rice

Hearts of Lettuce

Combination Salad

French, 1000 Island, Roquefort or Mayonnaise Dressing

Blueberry Cobbler a la Mode — Orange Sherbet

Butterscotch Sundae — Jellied Peach Chantilly

Orange Frosted Angel Cake — Assorted Cookies

Vanilla, Chocolate Ice Cream

Old English Cheddar — Bleu

Crackers

Tea — Coffee — Sanka — Postum — Buttermilk — Milk — Skim Milk

MEAL HOURS — Breakfast 8-9:30; Mid-day 12:30-1:30; Evening 6:30-8

BEVERAGE AND FOOD SERVICE

BIRD ROOM

CONTINENTAL BREAKFAST — 9:30 a.m.

ADIRONDACK ROOM

BEVERAGE SERVICE — 4:30 p.m. - 12:00 Midnight

FOOD SERVICE — A la Carte 9:30 p.m. - 12:00 Midnight

BOTTLE SERVICE — Call Ext. 756.

Dining Room Beverage Service

A selection of choice wines, champagnes and beers is available during mid-day and evening meals upon request from the wine waiters.

DAILY EVENTS

*Instruction in Skiing and Skating.

10&2 Mt. Whitney. *Ski School Classes.

12:00 Mt. Whitney Ski Loj. Lunch served. Obtain meal transfer ticket from head waiter during breakfast.

4:30 Garth Lounge. Afternoon Tea.

6:00 Adirondack Room. *Cocktail Hour.

6:30 Adirondack Room. Dancing.

7:45 Garth Lounge. Coffee Hour.

9:00 Adirondack Room. Dancing - Paul Jouard and his Orchestra.

Thursday, February 22, 1968

8.45 Agora. *Motion Picture. "The King and I" with Yul Brynner and Deborah Kerr.

Friday, February 23, 1968

10.00 Mt. Van Hoevenberg. *North American Bobsled Championships.

3.00 Club Rink. Sno Bird Skating Gymkhana. Sno Bird ribbons for winners.

9.00 Agora. *Ski Film Feature: Dick Barrymore's great production of "A Cool Breath of Fresh Air" and The FIS Championships in Chile with Jean Claude Killy.

10.00 Adirondack Room. The "SONNETEERS" of Skidmore College in a program of songs.

**Events starred require cash expenditure*

Mid-day Menu 1968 CAMPBELL COLLECTION

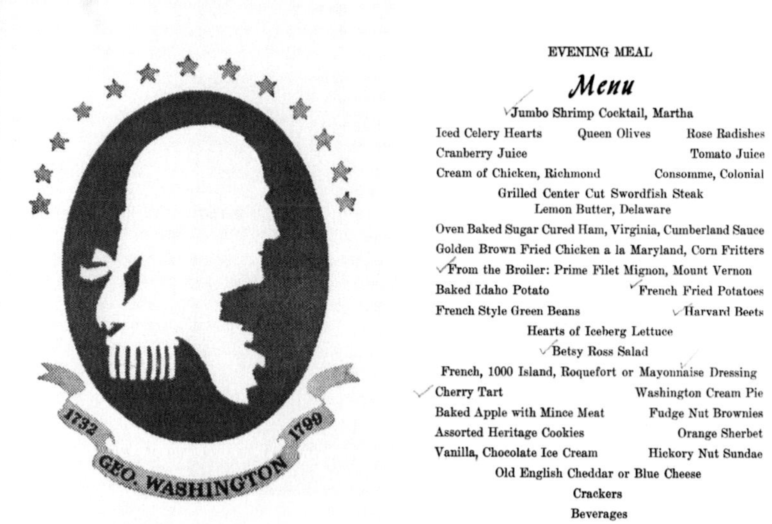

EVENING MEAL

Menu

Jumbo Shrimp Cocktail, Martha

Iced Celery Hearts — Queen Olives — Rose Radishes

Cranberry Juice — Tomato Juice

Cream of Chicken, Richmond — Consomme, Colonial

Grilled Center Cut Swordfish Steak

Lemon Butter, Delaware

Oven Baked Sugar Cured Ham, Virginia, Cumberland Sauce

Golden Brown Fried Chicken a la Maryland, Corn Fritters

From the Broiler: Prime Filet Mignon, Mount Vernon

Baked Idaho Potato — French Fried Potatoes

French Style Green Beans — Harvard Beets

Hearts of Iceberg Lettuce

Betsy Ross Salad

French, 1000 Island, Roquefort or Mayonnaise Dressing

Cherry Tart — Washington Cream Pie

Baked Apple with Mince Meat — Fudge Nut Brownies

Assorted Heritage Cookies — Orange Sherbet

Vanilla, Chocolate Ice Cream — Hickory Nut Sundae

Old English Cheddar or Blue Cheese

Crackers

Beverages

Evening Menu, Washington's Birthday 1968 CAMPBELL COLLECTION

Flower window off Bird Room by entrance to Dining Room, February 1968. CAMPBELL PHOTO

Marguerite and Gordon K. Campbell, the author's parents in the Bird Room, 1972. Father is in daytime dress. At dinner he became the proper banker he was in 3 piece suit, white shirt and tie. CAMPBELL PHOTO

CHAPTER 7

One Hell of a Cold but Clear of Dope, and a Club Birth

Telephone operators talk all the time. Millie Kelly's voice was raspy from bronchitis when she asked for the names of incoming guests at the front desk. Dr. George Hart heard her and let out a hoot that could be heard clear to Keene (10 miles away), "You've got one hell of a cold! Get right down to my office!" - which Kelly did!

Throughout the Club's 85 years there was always professional medical care on staff available to members, and in later years, to employees. The Club was adamant in Club Notes from at least Sept. 1905 that "the Club physician has the right to exclude tuberculosis cases from staying at the Club." By Sept. 1908 there was a Club pharmacist, G. B. Merriam.

From June 24 to Sept. 15, 1909, the Club infirmary had 14 medical patients, five surgical patients and 130 day treatment cases. There were four operations. The average stay in the infirmary was 6.8 days. There were six nurses and three attendants.

Dr. A. C. Burnham was Associate Club Physician from July 1 through Sept. 30, 1911 and had 17 medical cases and five surgical cases (three operations)

The Club boasted to members in Oct. 1912, "A prominent New York physician and surgeon of over 20 years practice is in residence all the year. The Club infirmary has an operating room and contagious ward for emergencies. Danger from tuberculosis is rigidly excluded, the verdict of the Club physician being final in any doubtful case."

It was reported in Club Notes that on Jan. 4, 1914 Dr. Charles Ross Jackson, for nearly three years resident Club physician, died suddenly of angina pectoris (according to Dewey) at his home in Lake Placid.

Annie Godfrey Dewey, Melvil's first wife, conferred in 1908 with experts at the Battle Creek Sanitarium about her own health and was told she had but a few months to live because of the hardening of the arteries. According to the tribute to Annie Dewey by the Journal of Home Economics, she had not the slightest fear of death but told Melvil, "I shall be sorry to leave you alone but if I can't work longer here I should like to get my next job started over there." She lived for 15 more years.

Annie Dewey traveled in January 1914 to Battle Creek, Michigan, to the first National Conference on Race Betterment. Mrs. Dewey presented an address, quite lengthy, on "Euthenics and Its founder, Mrs. Ellen H. Richards", a professor at Massachusetts Institute of Technology.

The following summer, Club Notes July-August 1914 reported that "Club graduate nurse Mrs. Cornelia Anderson, for five years was one of the best nurses in the famous Battle Creek Sanitarium where she had thorough training and long experience in both Swedish and German massage and various baths and special treatments for which Battle Creek is the recognized leader. She is the permanent Club nurse. Her services are available for massage and special treatments and part-time professional help at $1.00 per hour."

The economy and convenience of Club medical care was stressed in May 1916. "The Club has one or more nurses in residence all the year to save delay and the heavy expense of bringing an expert nurse from the city (New York) to whose salary of $25 a week, travel time, railroad and Club bills must be added. Total expenses often amount to $100 a week when a nurse is brought from a distance. The Club nurse will never cost more than $6 a day."

Nov. 1916 Club Notes state that Dr. William George Russell had taken up permanent residency as Club physician, health officer and medical director. "He specialized in diseases and development of children and in adults who are run down and below par. He has seen the best results coming often with little or no use of drugs, health and strength being restored quicker by carefully planned and supervised diet, exercise, Nauheim electric light and other special baths and massages." With this family of 1,700 (1000 guests and 700 employees) the trustees voted that an expert Medical Director must be constantly supervising all matters of sanitation, watching carefully for contagious diseases. One of the first duties of the Medical Director was again to exclude any guest who had tuberculosis or any other disease that might imperil or annoy others.

Improvements for 1917 noted that the Medical Director's office was equipped with the latest X-ray, electric and other apparatus.

For the summer of 1917 Club dentist Dr. T. E. Sherlock would open a completely equipped modern office next door to the medical director's office on the ground floor of Forest Towers.

Club Notes relate that in 1918, influenza struck the village and farms, though the Club escaped. There were 43 deaths or five times as many as from World War I for the Village. When the railroad was at its height, there were two big old hotels across from the train station, the National House and the American House. One of them was taken over in 1919 and converted to a temporary hospital to accommodate people who were suffering from the flu epidemic.

It was proudly again reported in Club Notes in April 1918 that the Club pharmacy was the largest and best of the four local drugstores. In 1928 the pharmacy was improved and enlarged.

All of this medical concern for Club members did not extend equally to employees and frequently in the early days as with so many things, Club employees relied on themselves and helped each other. Anne Florence Marshall, wife of Gordon R. Marshall, often skated across Mirror Lake to go shopping. She was pregnant in February 1919, when she fell on the ice which contributed to the premature birth of Karen Peter's uncle Donald. Karen's aunt, Tyne Marshall, who was a trained nurse, and another woman who lived in the Annex and who had had two premature births of her own attended Karen's grandmother. Her uncle weighed in at 5 pounds. The women put him in a clothes basket with pillows, hot water bottles and bathed him in olive oil. Karen's grandmother nursed him without even picking him up. Donald Marshall always claimed to be one of the few children ever born at the Lake Placid Club. (Peter's letters 2-22 & 7-7-02)

For the employees, on May 31,1927 the Club offered benefits of group insurance at the rate of 50 cents per $1,000 per month. Employees who had been on staff for one or more years were eligible and showing employee concern for their own health, 83% of eligible staff applied for the insurance. The maximum policy was $3,600 and the minimum $800, face amount payable in case of death or permanent disability before the age of 60.

In June 1921 records show that "Dr. Louise C. Ball of New York, whose work in preventive dentistry so interested members last summer, will be installed in the same office this season. In 1916 she founded courses for women in dental hygiene assisted by the Rockefeller Foundation, was for two years dean of dental courses at Columbia University and has conducted examinations for dentists under the New York Municipal Civil Service commission."

In 1921 Dr. A. R. Grant, consulting surgeon connected with Utica Hospital, served the Club.

In May 1929, D. C. Munro, M.D., a physician of Utica became Club medical director in year round residence. The medical unit had therapeutic, sitz and cabinet baths, ultra violet and infra red lamps, an electric sine-wave generator, and Battle Creek muscle building and reducing machines.

The August 1944 report of Samuel H. Packer to the annual meeting of the Lake Placid Club gathered in Agora discussed the use of the Club as a redistribution center by the Army. The advantage was it kept the staff together to operate properties and facilities for Army use. He strongly reiterated that the Club would not be a hospital or used for convalescents. Beginning Sept. 8, 1944 the Army would need living accommodations and food for 200. In less than two weeks, they needed accommodations and food for 500. The entire premises were needed by Oct. 1, 1944.

Dr. George C. Owens served as Club physician after the Army left in 1945 until Dr. Hart was appointed in 1950. When Dr. Hart came, there was a masseur but not as sports medicine treatment. All the treatment rooms and equipment were gone.

Dr. Hart, born to a Club employee in 1916, started working at the Club himself as a caddy when he was about 10 years old. He also worked as a houseman, bellboy and in the Post Office when his father was Post Master. He went to medical school at McGill University, Montreal, Canada. Uncle Sam called in 1942 and he was 3 1/2 years in the Pacific including time on Iwo Jima. He started as a general practitioner in Lake Placid in 1946.

About 1950, Truman Wright, general manager of the Club, appointed Dr. Hart Club physician, a position he held until roughly

1980. Dr. Hart's main office was in the Village at 153 Main St. He had office hours at the Club every day until 11:00 a.m. and then made house calls. While Dr. Hart served as Club physician, he was also health director for the Town of North Elba, Village of Lake Placid. Dr. Hart gave up his practice in 1987 when he retired.

Dr. Hart related the history of medical care in Lake Placid as he told that Dr. Proctor's home on the corner of Mirror Lake Dr. and Parkside, across from the Village tennis courts, was bought and converted into a general hospital until Placid Memorial Hospital was opened in 1951. This closed as an acute care hospital and merged with Saranac Lake Hospital. In contrast to Lake Placid which was and is known as a sports center, Saranac Lake was a health resort and the Trudeau Sanitarium was over there. Many of the houses in Saranac Lake were tuberculosis cure cottages.

A good portion of the medical care for guests at the Club was of elderly people with various illnesses, including heart attacks and strokes. When John Watt was Club manager, Dr. Hart said he needed a wheelchair to use when people had fainted. Watt said, "No wheelchairs." A wheel chair could give the appearance of the dreaded sanitarium.

When someone died at the Club, Dr. Hart insisted on informing Watt immediately even if it was in the middle of the night. After all, that person would not be at breakfast or able to check out! Dr. Hart delivered many babies in the Village but delivered no babies at the Club. Dr. Hart received no salary from the Club. He had the privilege of being the doctor on call for the Club and had an office in the Club. Members and guests paid for their treatment at the Club. In return, Dr. Hart took care of the Club employees, free.

In Dr. Hart's day, there was a dental office at the Club but it was space rented to a dentist, not run by a Club Dentist.

If Club guests didn't ski Whiteface Mt., they skied Mt. Whitney, which the Club owned. At first there were a lot of ankle injuries but as ski boots developed, stiff ski boots encased the ankle and the injuries were then higher up in the leg. Dr. Hart used lots of plaster in making casts for broken limbs. He never used the plastic casts or removable casts held with velcro so common now since these were not of his time period. More complicated fractures (those difficult to align) would be sent to a general surgeon.

The practice of medicine, from one point of view, stayed the same throughout Dr. Hart's 30 years at the Club. That was his relationship with his patients. Dr. Hart's simple statement was, "I'd be available to them." When patients called, he saw them the same or the next day. He didn't give them an appointment in two weeks. Former patients still tell him, "I wish you'd go back into practice again."

Other things did change radically in those 30 years. As Dr. Hart recalled the advent of antibiotics changed the practice of medicine. Penicillin was new in the 1930s and 40s. It was available in Army hospitals but not in the field. It became the drug of choice for upper respitorary problems and colds after World War II. It also became a much overused drug. Germs became resistant to it, people developed allergies to it. Erythromycin and other related drugs followed, again resulting in overuse.

The pattern of diseases changed. Dr. Hart saw cases of cancer of the stomach when he first started. That lessened perhaps due to a change in eating habits, a decrease in fats and meats and increase in fruits and vegetables but there was an increase in pancreatic cancer.

The use of X-rays changed as CAT scans, and MRIs were unknown. Machinery had not been developed for them. Older

X-rays could give a picture of the spine, newer ones get down into the spinal cord now.

Trauma surgery is now a specialty and nuclear medicine did not exist in Dr. Hart's practice. There are now more definitive heart drugs and surgery.

Economic factors impacted the practice of medicine also. Many of the doctors in northern New York are graduates of McGill University in Montreal. It was natural for these doctors, Dr. Hart included, to refer patients to hospitals in Montreal as they had trained there and knew the doctors and facilities. These referrals dropped off precipitously when the advent of socialized medicine in Quebec meant American patients were expected to make cash payment upon entrance to the hospital.

Dr. Hart was in solo practice. Today group practice is the norm. Dr. Hart's house call was $10. Today doctors are finding they can bill Medicare $180 for a house call. (Wall Street Journal, 8-2-02). Today's doctors are faced with malpractice premiums of $150,000 before they see their first patient.

Placid Memorial Hospital served Dr. Hart's patients quickly and well. When it closed, it meant an eight-mile trip to Saranac Lake. The hospital there has a helicopter. More serious cases were flown to Burlington, VT.

Calling 911 did not exist during the life of the Club. Dr. Hart would be called for ski accidents. If an ambulance was needed, one would be called. Ambulances were owned and run by Mr. Clark, the funeral director.

In the 1932 Winter Olympics, Hart was in the parade of athletes carrying a Canadian flag. During the 1980 Winter Olympics, Dr. Hart was on the Medical Commission of the International Olympic Committee representing Lake Placid. He was in charge of medical services, organizing medical care at the several Olympic sites. He missed the Russian/American hockey game because he was in his office treating about 20 ABC network staff members who had the flu. The Russian doctor did congratulate Dr. Hart when the Americans won the hockey game and the gold medal. He still sends Dr. Hart a Christmas card, as does the Japanese doctor. In those 1980 Winter Olympics, there were no doping violations discovered. In Dr. Hart's words, "We were clear of dope."

The Lake Placid Club Postmark CAMPBELL ARCHIVE

CHAPTER 8

Steam Heat, Washing Udders and Soap Suds

Power and Construction

The Club, in its self-sufficiency, could be compared to a trans-atlantic ocean liner or to a city unto itself. The Club power house generated the steam to heat all its buildings– cottages, three Clubhouses, activity and maintenance facilities, and the green houses for year round flowers. The Club laundry and dry cleaning operation were commercial operations. Club farms supplied milk and food. The meat market sold prime cuts, the General Store sold sundries and U.S. mail arrived at the Club Post Office.

Bob Sweeney, who had first worked at General Electric and had been in the Navy, started working in the Power House in 1948. Twelve men worked there, one Chief Engineer and eleven shift workers, three per shift. The steam equipment was Norberg and Skinner steam engines and a Babcock and Wilcox oil fired boiler. The exhaust steam was sent through pipes to heat the buildings, some of which were 1 1/2 miles away from the power house.

In the summer the laundry used some of the steam but much of the stream had to be blown off, therefore wasted. Think of the expression, "He's just blowing off steam", meaning, "Don't listen to him. He's not serious about what he's saying." Steam blown off doesn't produce energy.

The Club burned coal,18 tons of coal a day in cold weather according to Melvil Dewey (Club Notes June 1917). Later examples from the Lake Placid Club Power Reports are for the years 1944-1956. Then the Club consumed an average of 6,148 tons a year, the most being 7,057 tons in 1945 when the Army was at the Club. Between November 1956 and October 1957, the Club consumed 6,310 tons of coal for a yearly cost of $73,987.12. In January 1957, because the average temperature was eight degrees, 790 tons were consumed at a cost of $9,247 for that month. Even summer months in the Adirondacks required hot water and some steam heat. The July 1957 average temperature was 61 degrees and 442 tons were consumed for a monthly cost of $5,196.

Then the Club switched to bunker #6 oil. It cost 7 cents a gallon; the oil cost 3 cents and the delivery charge was 4 cents. When the oil price increased to 90 cents a gallon, the process was too expensive and a total loss. "If you use the steam, it's not bad," explained Sweeney.

In December 1948, the Club began to use village water for the power house, laundry, Westgate group and for cold water in Agora. The new power plant of the 1950s was nice and clean but it became cheaper to buy electricity from the Village of Lake Placid. After Feb. 22, 1961, the power house crew was cut back to a six man operation – Chief Engineer and five men for a savings of $20,000 a year.

Bob Sweeney worked under other chief engineers; a previous one was fired and Guy Stevenson, Superintendent of Plant, asked Sweeney to take over until he could get another engineer. Sweeney said he didn't want to but he would. "How long would it be?"

"A month or two" was the response. After that time, Sweeney asked when the new engineer was coming. Stevenson said, "I'm looking at him." Sweeney then got his engineer's license.

During the Club's last stand, they put in two small boilers in the main building, which were too small, not efficient and not the right steam pressure. They held only 13 lb. pressure, while the big boilers could reduce from 250 lb. to 30 lb. pressure in the power house.

Just before the 1980 Olympics, when the survival of the Club was in real question, one of the last managers of the Club told Sweeney he was having men from the Hilton come over to supervise the power house. They came and saw the little boilers being used then. Sweeney and the superintendent of plant were called to the manager's office and told that the fellows from the Hilton would not be supervising. After seeing the equipment, they wanted no responsibility. The manager was worried about the power house and asked Sweeney what he should do. Sweeney told him, "You go home and watch the Olympics on TV!"

After Sweeney retired, the superintendent of plant wanted him to do plumbing work. He was a steam fitter and not a plumber but he became head plumber. He fixed all steam lines, and worked wherever there was trouble, be it in rooms or the dishwasher in the kitchen. Wherever there were major problems, the plumbers got around them.

The Club carpenters in the early days constantly constructed and repaired. Club Notes in Jan-Feb 1915 state, "Members may have sleeping balconies built (on cottages or clubhouses) where not architecturally objectionable by paying half the cost". A year later, Club Notes announced, "...we are building this year suites from 1 - 11 rooms with baths, balconies, open fire places, etc., just to suit. Your wants can be met for 1916 if you apply at once." If members preferred to keep a car at the cottage so it could be used on a moment's notice, Club Notes in June of 1916 said, "...on three days notice we will build a garage adjoining any cottage."

When the Club was growing, Ed Richards, father of Mary Wallace, was a foreman of the carpenter shop. Her uncle, Ezra Richards, was foreman of outside labor. They worked on building the T bar ski lift and the bobsled run on Club property. From 1966 to 1984, Allen Lawrence worked at the Club year round as a carpenter. He did shop work: making screens, doors, cabinets and remodeling. In his time, there was no new construction and major work was let out to contract. Lawrence worked at the Mt. Whitney Ski Lodge building a bar and spent all of one summer at the top of the ski lift building ramps. Club buildings not used for the winter had to be boarded up even though they were checked daily. It took two months in the spring to get things open. Lawrence likes doing any kind of carpentry work – whatever needs to be done.

The carpenter shop, new in 1970, had every kind of power tool – table saws, planes, band saws, mortise presses, and lathes. In the same area as the carpenter shop were the print shop where the daily menus and other Club printing was done; the paint shop, cabinet shop, plumbing shop, electric shop and the warehouse for plumbing and other supplies. In the words of Bob Sweeney, "We all got along good and helped each other out."

Virginia Gilmore's father, Robert Lacey, was a maintenance person who did other jobs in town. If he needed work, he would go to the Club and most of the time the Club would put him on.

Club employees manned saws to harvest a material other than wood for the pleasure of Club members. In the winter, before the days of refrigeration, 6,000,000 pounds of ice from Lake Placid would be cut and stored in ice houses to keep the Club family of 1,400 supplied with ice in August.

Herdsires and Daughters

Given its isolated upstate location, it was logical for the Club to buy farms to assure a steady supply of fresh quality food for members and guests. Before World War I the Club had almost 600 head of cattle – Guernseys, Jerseys, Ayrshires and Holsteins. For many a Club employee, a career at the Club started on Pinebrook Farm as a barn man which meant washing the udders of the Ayrshires with warm water before milking, and cleaning the stables. Great pride was taken in that farm's having the lowest bacteria count of other farms in the county.

George Beauregard was brought up in an orphanage run by the Brothers of Charity in Roxbury, Mass. At age 16, they lined up the boys, chose George and pinned a train ticket on him. He was sent to Averyville to watch over a woman who was going blind. When George was 18 in 1923, the neighbor on the Club Averyville farm next door said he needed a man and would hire George for board plus $30 a month. For three years George was in charge of breeding and did hand milking twice a day. There he met his first wife who was working on the farm for $3 a week.

Virginia Gilmore's house in Wildwood is where the Averyville farm cows were watered. Her grandfather, Harrison Lawrence, was the Club buttermaker around 1910. During an early flu epidemic (not the big one in 1919), he worked all day and took Virginia's mother with him, going from farm to farm milking by hand for farmers downed by the flu. Cows need to be milked and he was the only one not sick.

In 1914, the creamery took first prize at the State Dairyman's Association in New York and Pennsylvania. It was also a prize winner on Neufchatel cheese. Part of the Club history is the farm employees trying out milking machines on the Holstein farms and after two years of trials, purchasing them. Milking machines allowed two men to do the work of three.

The creamery made both sherbets and ice cream. Peppermint ice cream was made at Christmas. Some think French vanilla was the best to make and the best to eat. In 1942, 3,893 gallons were produced. Mary Wallace recalls that when not all of the ice cream was used at the Club and it was to be thrown out, the fellow taking it to the dump would stop at her house. Everybody in the neighborhood knew when the big cylinders were dropped off and came to Mary's house to especially enjoy the maple walnut ice cream. "Oh, it was fun! Nothing was ever wasted back in those days!"

In 1923, on the 40 farms owned by the Club, there were 116 horses, 486 cattle, 9,000 chickens and 416 pigs all cared for by Club employees. The food director was Ida Mae Hait who was "doing splendid work supervising the planning of menus, purchasing for the Club Store and balancing this with supplies from our farms." (Club Notes Summer 1926) Fresh vegetables came to the dining room tables from the Club farms and the potato harvest was particularly significant. Or significant, at least, for Jack Kendrick. He could get out of school for the potato harvest season and do hard, dirty work for 7 cents a bushel. For the chicken farms there was an incubator that held 3,600 eggs with a hatch of 2,200 every three weeks. These single comb white leghorn pullets would begin laying in July. Rhode Island Reds were bred for broilers as were white Peking ducks.

The reality of fire affected the farms, especially hay lofts, and kept Club carpenters busy. "We rebuilt the burned pig parlor and Holstein stable much better than before." (Club Notes Dec. 1918)

Audrey Pratt, mother of Beverly Reid, was a chambermaid at the Club. At the Averyville farm there was a pig pen where, in 1939 or 1940, the Club garbage was taken as slop for the pigs. Except it wasn't just garbage! Beverly, who doesn't like animals, was put by her mother over the fence in with the pigs and told, "Look at that dish over there. Go get that one, Beverly. And there's some silverware over there, go get that." They'd take it home, scrub it up, clean it and take it to camp. The Club's accidentally discarded Syracuse china became their camp dishes. When her family closed their camp, she doesn't know what happened to the silverware and dishes. Today there's a gorgeous house where the pig pen was and Beverly would like to ask the people, "Oh, do you know where you're living?"

The farm director, Favor Smith, reported in November 1941 that there were 272 head of cattle, and livestock sales amounted to $5,000, with culls sold at good figures to butchers or cattle dealers. Fair quality purebreds and better grades sold for $75 to $130, some as high as $175. The Jersey herd was at the Highland Farm, 88 purebreds and five of better grades. "The old 'Proven Herdsire' is still continuing to work and a large percentage of his daughters in the herd is helping to improve the appearance of the herd as well as increase production," wrote Smith.

At Pinebrook, "A proven Ayrshire herdsire was purchased last spring. He is one of about 30 'approved' Ayrshire bulls now living in the world as rated by the Ayrshire Association. He has 27 daughters."

According to Smith, "Good or poor quality labor may prove the limiting factor for good or poor production and health in the various herds in 1942. Cheap help with good cows is expensive," emphasized Smith in his report.

The production of Placid Brand certified seed potatoes still continued to be the best bet to make LPCo Farms a profitable venture. Bushels harvested numbered 35,000, a high yield of 459 bushels per acre. Placid Brand seed potatoes are sold in Massachusetts, New Jersey and Long Island. Some sent to central N.Y. State brought the comment, "I have never been able to buy seed as disease-free as Placid Brand." The Club received a request for one bushel for experimental purposes from Maine.

With hay, oats, hogs and poultry, the farms in the early 1940s were in the best workable shape that they had been in in a long time.

Snap the Sheets

Keeping bed linens, towels and guest clothes clean was a major operation where a good house meant 1,200 guests. One July during a tennis tournament, the laundry did 3,500 towels a day.

In the laundry wash room, where the men worked, there were three washers that could hold 300 lb.; one 200 lb. washer and two 50 lb. washers. Laundry went through two wash cycles and three rinse cycles. A washer formula (detergent) was used and clothes were sorted by color. There were three extractors for drying clothes, one big one, a couple of 100 lb. ones and two smaller extractors.

The women worked in the ironing room with four presses for uniforms, dresses and skirts, a shirt press for sleeves, collars and cuffs, and two for flat work - an eight roll press and a six roll press.

"It was a hot job!" remembered Marjorie Stevens who worked in the laundry from age 16 in 1948 through 1952. There was a hand ironing department as well as the mangles [ironing machines for flat work]. A stand up job was putting wet sheets through the mangle. They had to be folded right side out and if you had a good partner (as Stevens did in Peg Nugent), you could get a good rhythm going and "snap the sheets" before feeding them through the mangle.

Stevens worked May through September and went on unemployment in the winters. The shift was from 8 a.m. to 4 p.m. with a 10 minute break in the morning, break for lunch and a 10 minute break in the afternoon. Working conditions were strict. If you were talking, then you weren't working. The bathroom was downstairs and girls were timed if it was thought they took too long!

Mary Wallace folded things for the dining room. "You always had to fold napkins in three. A real official napkin is folded with no edges showing. To this day I still fold my linen napkins in."

Frances Silleck worked in the laundry half of one summer but her heart was in golf! (See Chapter 4)

The printery produced 350,000 menus a year in addition to other programs and brochures. The serious illness of Mr. Grady, Club printer, caused the Club to think of leasing the Printery to Barton Press in Lake Placid.

Henry Bonsignore had the barbershop concession starting in the late 1920s for the next 30 years. When the beauty shop was changing hands, he took it over also according to his daughter, Cornelia. Bonsignore had contact with all the men of the Club and established personal relationships with them. Gaetana (Tillie) Bonsignore, Cornelia's mother, worked in housekeeping making sure the linens were in order. The couple gathered Club furniture throughout the season that was in need of repair. During the slow time in winter, they would repair and re-upholster it. Tillie helped Kate Smith with curtains and interior decoration of her camp on Lake Placid.

Before Tillie came to Lake Placid, she was a custom tailoress. Her husband would take the men's measurements, she would make the patterns and then she would make silk shirts for men. Club Manager Henry Wade Hicks was a big man (six feet, four inches tall, 220 lbs) who had trouble getting clothes to fit so Tillie would make patterns and make his silk shirts and underclothes to order. Tillie took over the tailoring and dry cleaning for the Club after the Army left. The Club dry cleaning equipment was set up but had not been used until after the Army left in 1945. When the Army was stationed at the Club in January of 1945, officers' and enlisted men's uniforms were dry cleaned for 75 cents. Fancy wool dresses of Army wives or dependant civilian employees were cleaned for 40 cents, men's suits for $1.50, women's two piece dresses for $2.25, swagger suits for $2.50. Staff prices were one half of guest prices. During the war, dry cleaning was sent out to Krinivitz Cleaners and Spiegels Dry Cleaning in Plattsburg.

Downstairs under the laundry, in dry cleaning after the war, there was a 100 lb. dry cleaning washer. At the spotting machine, an attendant who knew what chemicals to use with which materials put them on the spot and used an air gun to go over the stains. The clothes were put in the washer and then pressed. They did men's suits, summer white suits, and ladies dresses.

The Club had a still and the revenuers knew about it! The United States Treasury Dept notified the Club in January of 1946 that "Information (was) received you have purchased a still Serial #4511168 from American Laundry Machinery Co. It must be registered." (Maybe the Army did detective work while they were there!) The Club still (not for Club parties!) was "for reclaiming dry cleaning solvents" at the new laundry which went into operation June 1946.

Victor Bonsignore, son of Henry and Tillie, was the dry cleaning valet throughout his high school years picking up and delivering dry cleaning. There was a truck to pick up and deliver clothes to the cottages but some guests brought the clothes in. The usual turnaround time on laundry and dry cleaning for guests was two to three days. If they wanted it "done special", meaning the guest needed it for that night or the next morning, 25% was added to the bill. Guests had clean clothes when they wanted them. There was a lot of activity in the laundry during the annual Horse Show. The guests wanted it "done special" to get rid of the horsey smells!

CHAPTER 9

Christmas, Conventions, Council Fires, Terminated: No Bra

Jobs, Jobs, Jobs

From a town perspective, the Club was jobs - large and small. The Club was a local employer with multiple needs and it offered jobs of all kinds.

Edward Hart, father of Dr. George Hart, worked at the General Store six days a week, 8 a.m. to 6 p.m. as head of the grocery department. When Hart and his wife had a new baby his wages were $15 a week and employees wouldn't get paid from one fall until the next spring. He needed $50 to get through the winter. He went to Melvil Dewey, explained his situation and asked for $100. Melvil lived up to his reputation of cutting a request by half and said, "Well, do you think you could get along on fifty?

Hart said, "I'll try."

Melvil Dewey said, "I'll give you fifty", which is exactly what Hart wanted.

Dewey also assessed the climate and told Hart, "You know, Lake Placid will never have a good winter or a bad summer." Winters were sparce then as far as tourists went and resulted in seasonal employment for many until the Club introduced winter sports.

The blacksmith Patrick McKeon had a forge and bellows at the Club. He raised iron to white heat, molded horse shoes and took them to the Club drivery to be fit to horses. The drivery was run by Fred Douglass.

There was a butcher shop and freight office where all the trunks and freight for the Club were brought from the train station.

The United States Weather Bureau station at the Club opened New Year's Day in 1909. The official records on the government instruments were the responsibility of Henry van Hoevenberg, chief engineer. Van Hoevenberg owned the Adirondack Lodge, a log structure built in 1878-80 that accommodated 60 guests. He operated it until the forest fire of 1903 when he got the horses out, "...dropped the silverware and other valuables in the shallow water of Heart Lake and fled..." (Ackerman 67). Melvil Dewey took van Hoevenberg in and he did engineering and electrical work at the Club. The Olympic bobsled run and mountain are named for "Mr. Van." The Adirondack Loj (Dewey's spelling) owned since 1959 by the Adirondack Mountain Club and accommodating 24 guests is on the site of Mr. Van's original lodge.

George Marshall, Karen Peter's great-grandfather was Head Stone Mason at the Club in the early 1900s. He built most of the stone fireplaces and continued to work at the carpenter shop and mill.

Melvil Dewey reported to members in <u>Club Notes</u> Sept 1908 that there was a 94 foot chimney on the then new power house. He gleefully added that members should "ask the engineer to open the damper a few seconds, then stand in front of the open door if you are not afraid of being pulled up the 48 inch flue." Gordon R. Marshall, who also was a mason, and an engineer in the power house had to shovel coal into that furnace and he was not gleeful when he went home with singed hair. He learned the electrician's trade at the Club, did bellhopping, left in 1922 and worked for General Electric. Until 1922 he and his wife, Anne Florence Wilkins Marshall lived in the Annex. Gordon was an avid sportsman and excelled in hunting, fishing, skiing and ice skating. He was an ice-skating instructor at the Club skating rink (tennis courts in summer). He set up the skating rink and kept it in good skating order, which he accomplished by flooding it with hot water from the boiler room to make the ice smooth. He also maintained the hockey rink (or "box"). He was in charge of the nightlights on the rink. One time he jumped the hockey fence, got his chin caught in the wiring and landed on the ice, resulting in a concussion.

Richard Bonsignore worked at the Club in the 19teens through 1920s. Summers he worked at the boathouse but winters his unique Christmas vacation job was to get up at 4 a.m., walk across Mirror Lake from home and get the leather ski boots of the guests. He would oil the boots and get them back to the guests before they woke up.

As concessionaires, the Bonsignores had guest privileges and got to meet Lowell Thomas, Ted Collins and in particular, Ted's daughter. Richard would accompany her to Club events. Richard went to New York University and worked for a Club member in accounting. He went into the service, and was Comptroller for General Dynamics and then a stockbroker.

In 1922, Margaret Dawson's hairdressing rooms offered six operators who used the latest electric equipment for permanent waves and marceling.

Raymond McIntyre worked at the Post Office but his father, the Post Master, was a tough boss! This was the Club's own United States Post Office with P.O. boxes in the Lobby. The mail came in by train three times a day. The Club Mailman drove the mail truck to the station to get it. McIntryc had to sort it and put it in guests' mail boxes. Special Delivery mail had 25 cents postage on it and was delivered to guests' rooms. Ray then received 9 cents a letter from the government for that service.

The Lake Placid High School Class of 1935 graduation was at the Club because the high school was under construction. Araxie Dunn was a member of that class. Her mother was Armenian and worked to raise money in town and through speeches at the Club for Armenian Relief, needed because of the genocide of Armenians in 1915 by the Turks. Henry Wade Hicks, Club manager, encouraged Dunn's mother to go into business for herself since she spent so much time raising money for others. They opened a gift shop in the house where they lived on Mirror Lake which is now part of the Lake Placid Public Library. Melvil Dewey would send people to her shop. There was an electric boat that would hold 8 people that the Club ran for people to go overtown to shop.

Elizabeth Wilson worked in the Club drugstore in 1949 through 1951. The drugstore, jewelry shop, and photographer were in space within the Club leased from the Lake Placid Company. Her husband, Cal, as a bellhop and busboy, worked for the Lake Placid Club. Elizabeth, working for a concessionaire, had more privileges than Cal did. The drugstore was located in Garth Lounge where the tea was served and where the string quartet played. One member would bring afternoon tea and cookies to Elizabeth. Someone criticized this member who explained her action was appropriate as Elizabeth was an employee of the Company and had higher rank than Club employees.

The brothers of Psi U fraternity at Wesleyan University, Middletown, Conn. were G-men for the Club. Howard Baker inherited one of these jobs which was to dance with the old ladies, call bingo, hand out programs at concerts and hymnals at chapel services. G-man? Gigolo, of course!

Personnel Policies

In 1940, there were 274 employees at Christmas time who had a total of 137 children. To be eligible for the gift check of $2, the following formula was used: Children whose 15th birthday had not arrived by Dec. 26th and either or both parents were employed by the Lake Placid Co. 10 months during the previous 12 were eligible to receive a gift. The children's gifts therefore totaled $274.

For the employees the amount of the bonus was determined by years of service. Those with 20 or more years received $5, 5 - 20 years $3, less than 5 years $2 and summer and winter not steadily throughout the year received $1. In 1940, this totaled $894.

Vacations were granted in 1933 to elected officers of the Club, clerks, stenographers and office workers and a list of employees in administrative capacities such as music director, kitchen director, "per capita" clerk, and farm director. After 10 months employment they were eligible for 2 weeks vacation, such credit not allowed to acculumate. No sick leave was allowed as a matter of right. The Vice President might, at his discretion, excuse absences caused by sickness of not more than one day if the work was made up.

Leases of Club housing were consistent in that the lease ceased upon termination of employment at the Club. The Club furnished the rental space, provided "staff linen", dishes and kitchen utensils, heat, hot water, stove and refrigerator, and garbage removal. The tenant was billed for electricity and telephone charges and the lessee agreed not to keep or house dogs, cats or other pets. One contract stated the family dog would be housed in a kennel in Lake Placid during the weekend visits of the employee's husband!

Employment at the Club was the real world and ended in termination for some. One notice of hearing before the New York State Department of Labor, Unemployment Insurance Referee Section, states "your employment...has been terminated as of July 14, 1962 due to your refusal to report to work." A waitress was informed by the Personnel Department on July 6, 1978, "that your manner of dress is not acceptable to the Lake Placid Club Resort's standards... As you have already been told about not wearing a bra in the dining room twice...this will be the last time that you will be asked. After you have read (and signed) this memo, we expect you to have a bra on, on your next shift. If not, then we feel that we can no longer employ you."

The Depression and 1932 Winter Olympics

The Club was a retreat from the outside world and all signs of business transactions were handled discreetly at the Front Desk. In October 1929, however, the Club relented. Although the requests to open a broker's office had always been declined, so many asked that one of the leading New York brokers was allowed to set up an office over the barbershop which adjoined the telegraph office, a step from the Front Desk yet entirely out of sight.

George Hatfield was caddying at the time of the Crash. Messages came out to the golfers who went inside and were never again seen at the Club. Mr. Colburn told Seymour Dunn, golf pro, that he would have to divide more of his sales income at the Golf House with the Club but Dunn wouldn't take that and left the Club for New York City and set up an indoor golf school. According to Araxie Dunn, Seymour's daughter-in-law, Lake Placid was hell during the Depression. If a woman didn't have a husband who was a hunter, fisher or a farmer with a root cellar, she was in trouble. Others have said that the Club Stores helped employee families make it through the Depression.

Dewey's statement that "We had our worst year 1930" was repeated in 1946 after the Army moved out. In June 1931 $38,000 was taken from the $2,500,000 Club Securities for operating costs. Club Manager Harry Hicks took on new duties of looking for new members as he traveled to Rochester; Pittsburgh; Hanover, N. H.; Hartford, Conn.; Philadelphia; and Morristown, N.J., to show movies and slides of the Club to friends of members of the Club. Other management personnel also toured the country promoting the Club for members, for employees and for college ski teams to compete at the Club.

Conventions of organizations with which the Deweys had a connection like the New York Library Association and the Home Economics Association had long relationships with the Club. The Club sought convention trade more aggressively as a result of the Depression. In 1931 the Colonnade Co. had a convention of 30 people for 10 days starting June 7. The convention of the New York State League of Savings and Loan Association brought 300 people June 16-18. Fifty representatives of Country Day Schools came June 25-27. Between 300 and 600 conventioneers came for the Library Association, School Superintendents and New York State Federation of Women's Clubs.

The International Assembly of Rotary International to educate incoming District Governors was teased away from Chicago and was held at the Club from 1949-1974. It was a 10 to 12 day event held in Agora. Rotary staff came two weeks early and worked with Howard Baker, convention director and later director of development, and Club staff to set up the Assembly. The color scheme was blue and gold. Each governor had to have exactly the same sized desk with equal access to the podium. Bob Reynolds remembers the seating charts and having to line the name cards up perfectly one way and then move 90 degrees and make sure they were lined up from that perspective. They were very particular about how things went. Some wanted ice water. Others wanted water with no ice. There was a translators' booth and each governor had a receiver so he could choose from simultaneous translations in four or five languages.

Meals for conventioneers were very different for Jim Sileo, executive chef. Club members sauntered in and dined slowly. Opening the Dining Room doors for conventioneers was like opening a cattle shoot. They rushed in, attacked the buffet tables and were out within an hour! There were theme dinners such as western food if the next regular Rotary Convention for members was to be in Denver, or an evening in Hawaii, or all German food.

When the Assembly got too big for Agora, which they loved, it had to be housed overtown as well as at the Club. Rotary offered to build a Convention Center at the Club where the shop and service buildings were and split the cost with the Club 50/50. The Club could use the facility when Rotary was not there. The Club had good food, break out rooms, good staff and audio visual aids, but no indoor pool which could be tolerated. Rotary had come to the Club for 25 consecutive years but the Club turned the offer down.

Rotary moved to Boca Raton for 1975-1984, and met in various places until they moved to Anaheim, Calif., in 1993 where it has been ever since.

The Rotary income was one third of the Club's annual budget.

Lake Placid Club was a restricted club but lifted the restriction against Jews and Blacks during conventions. For a while this kept the convention business for the Club but as consciousness raising succeeded, this became grounds for conventions *not* to be booked at the Club.

To the outside world, the 1932 Winter Olympics awarded to Lake Placid through the efforts of Dr. Godfrey Dewey, Melvil's son, meant competition of 17 countries in ski jumping, speed and figure skating, and bobsledding. Lake Placid's own Curtis and J. Hubert Stevens won gold in the two-man bobsledding. Two gold medals for speed skating also stayed in Lake Placid with Jack Shea. Shea was the father of James who was a Nordic skier in the 1964 Olympics in Innsbruck and grandfather of Jimmy Shea who won gold for skeleton in the 2002 Winter Olympics in Salt Lake City, making them the only three consecutive generation Winter Olympic family.

Inside the Club, Olympic spirit took over one and a half months after the Dec 26, 1931 death of the Club founder Melvil Dewey. For the Front Desk, Feb. 12, 1932 meant assigning 1,602 guests to their rooms. This included one guest who wouldn't accept that the Club was full. He insisted on coming and slept in one of the Medical department's treatment rooms! For housekeeping and laundry it meant having all that linen available, making all those beds and doing the laundry afterward. The kitchen organized double seatings in Forest Dining Room and served 4,176 meals. The same day 1,072 meals were served in the Adirondack Room where Club members who lived in Lake Placid ate.

It was also the day of the worst thaw and required snow to be shoveled by hand out of the woods and trucked to the outdoor events. The 1932 indoor Olympic Ice Arena was a Godsend as warm weather did not affect that indoor ice.

Fun Stuff

Each Labor Day staff put on a Masquerade in Agora for guests. Staff individually created their costumes. The show was frequently a spoof on the Club as characters were named Melvin Dontwe, founder; Door Bell, Wedding Bell, School Bell and Dumb Bell the Bellhops and Lawrence Tid Bit, an opera singer. Jack Kendrick was part of a group of ten who dressed in drag and called themselves "The Woes of Women": Miss Conduct, Miss Used, Miss Carriage, Miss Abused. There were prizes, food and always a lot of dancing. Guests had similar events for themselves but it seems the guests enjoyed the staff maquerade more.

Staff created a yearbook, a booklet called "The Placid Dish." The typists are named, it was not published by the printery but mimeographed. In 1938 it tells in verse of the wonderful time waitresses had at the Masquerade, the bellhop laments that he has to "Carry this to two-two-ten and I'm in room 16, I want a pen", the caddies with hoof and mouth disease - hoof it all day and talk it all night, and of Crawford Merkle, All-American Tray Boy who was caught in an elevator with one tray in and one tray out when the elevator door closed on him. Another side of employee life at the Club peeks out as the waiter wrote, "Say Jack, how about a game of tennis. We'll have just 10 minutes to play but that's all right....I've got a date to go swimming with Nettie this afternoon and then I'm playing golf with Bob. Hey, got a date for the staff dance yet? I'm all set. It's only 3 days off."

Sonny Thomas, son of Lowell Thomas, was at the Taft School in Connecticut when Howard Baker (previously mentioned "gigolo") was. Lowell Thomas' voice was known and heard around the world and it was thought if he announced that the Dalai Lama was scared of an invasion of Lhasa by the Chinese, there would be help for Tibet. Lowell Thomas, therefore, in 1949 went to Lhasa, took many rolls of color movie film and started to leave Tibet. While getting on a donkey to get down the trail to where his car was, Thomas fell off the donkey and broke his leg in more than one place. He came to the Club on crutches to recuperate.

Sonny brought the rolls of movie film to the Club and didn't know what to do with them. George Carroll told him and Baker to take it up to Carroll's film room at the Club, edit it into an 1 1/2 hour film and show it to Club members. While the film was being edited, Elizabeth Wilson remembers that every afternoon in Agora for a couple of hours there were colored movies of Tibet - a place no one had ever seen. That film became "Out of This World", which, with a sound track, was shown in New York City for a year.

During another visit, Lowell Thomas, who could describe anything, was put in a four- man bobsled at Mt. van Hoevenberg with a tape recorder strapped to his back. He was expected to describe the experience of rounding the curves named Shady, and the Zigzag - zigging, and zagging as the bobsled came down the run.

At the finish line the tape recorder was removed, rewound and the play button hit. The tape recorder was working well. There was silence at first and then a slow but distinctive, "Oh, my God!" and that was all. The bobsled run made even the great Lowell Thomas speechless.

Labor Intensive Events

Christmas required page after page of instructions for employees: "Dining Room – hot chocolate and coffee, crackers and doughnuts served to Waits [waitstaff] at 7:00 a.m. before starting to sing carols", "Housekeeping - 10 bingo tables arranged in pairs...to hold gifts...distributed at Guest Christmas tree", "Shop Service - four branches (spruce, balsam, white pine and red pine)", "Front Desk - Bellman ...to assist at Sno Bird [Dewey spelling] flag-raising ceremony", "Store Manager - candy, nuts, raisins, etc. for staff children's stockings to children's library by 9:30 a.m." and then hourly schedules for December 22-January 3rd.

Employee Children's Christmas parties were big events but fun. On Dec 26, 1924, 220 employee children gathered in Agora at 4:30 for one half hour of music by the Club trio and organist, followed by the hunt for Santa Claus, who was hidden in Agora Suites and found by the jingle of his bells. From his heavy pack he gave each child that stocking filled with candy, nuts and raisins and a savings account bank book on Bank of Lake Placid with a $2.00 nest egg that could not be withdrawn without the approval of the Club secretary until the owner was 21. It was intended that the Christmas money would be increased by caddy earnings and dimes earned for running errands, and be saved to pay for education expenses.

Council Fires were great events from 1903-1952. Club grounds extended to the entrances of Indian and Avalanche passes, the two highest peaks between these passes named Iroquois and Algonquin. "Each September, in the Moon of the Flaming Leaves in the heart of the forest, we repeat some of the solemn ceremonies observed centuries ago by our predecessors," (Dewey, G &

M) Ceremonies before the Fire varied yearly to include Raising Up Rites, Return of the Maize Maiden (required 40 corn stalks), Passing of the Warpole, Green Corn Dance (250 cornstalks), and Condolence. Only these parts changed from year to year. Chiefs of the Six Nations [played by Club members] each presented their claim to light the annual Council Fire of the League. The Great White Chief Tadudaho stated all reasons were good and all Six Nations should light the fire together in a symbol of unity. Melvil Dewey played the part of the Great White Chief. There was a cast of 120 but only 20 speaking parts.

Staff distributed scripts and six staff were waiting in Theanoguen to apply make-up. Seven pilot fires were placed along Iroquois trail from Mirror Lake through Brookwood Forest to the six lodge fires at Onondaga. Engine No. 6 was on duty to remove all danger of the fire's spreading.

The audience was to remain absolutely quiet with no visible artificial lighting. Since the audience for the Council Fire usually exceeded 1,000, this lighting problem was solved by staff's "burying a large tank of kerosene, under water pressure, with a small (swivel) nozzle low down on the side of the League fire away from the audience, so that the firekeeper could direct a steady stream of kerosene into the base of the fire, resulting in leaping yellow flames that, while preserving the effect of firelight, gave ample illumination." (Dewey, G & M)

Preparations assigned to the outside superintendent included the large central fire 12 to 14 ft high, five tepees, six tepee fires, 12 torches, 150 feet of hose, 10 gallons of kerosene, six barrels of kindling wood, two cords of wood 16" split for tepee fires, 1,200 wooden seats gathered from Arden and grounds, plumbers take care of kerosene needle valve and on and on. Costumes were shirts, leggings, headresses, black wigs and feathers and afterward the costumes were mended and laundered and properly dried to be put away. The Council Fire took place at 8 p.m. after everyone had had dinner but, oh yes, there were hot dogs, doughnuts and lemonade and "one boy should do nothing but serve cream and put sugar in the coffee as much is wasted when many people handle it" and for next year, paper spoons to stir the coffee! "Police should be directed to control noise of "overtown gang" that gathers in the bushes during the ceremony, awaiting a chance at the food or to see the ceremony. There are always disturbing yelps and laughs issuing from nearby bushes." This was determined disrespectful by both Melvil and Godfrey Dewey.

Jack Kendrick lived in Mohawk, dressed in a Mohawk Indian costume and walked to Theanoguen to wait for the call, "Oh Mohawks to the council fire." "O ye Onondagas, come forward." Araxie Dunn was very impressed with the Council Fires, "but it was held at the height of the bug season!"

Celebrities required special set-up work from the employees. Lowell Thomas' radio broadcast from the Club was relatively simple. But it was more complicated when Arthur Godfrey broadcast his television show from the Club, Feb. 20-24, 1956. Twenty-two to twenty five people were expected. Mr. Godfrey occupied Agora suite 521, 523 and 524 and he received room service.

In Forest East Suites, from where the show was telecast, staff removed the venetian blinds and hung draperies provided by the Chamber of Commerce. The heat was controlled at 70 degrees. All cars were removed from the parking area of the back road by Forest during the telecast.

In the Bird Room, the fireplace on the west side of the room was set by a houseman and left ready for firing. The ice skating rink was to be cleared and in perfect condition. The telephone crew was to install the necessary equipment for signal transmission.

Audrey Thornton came to Lake Placid in the mid-1970s because her daughter was a student at North Country School. Mr. John Watt, Club manager and a good friend, called her and said, "You're living in a house that's half built. Would you like to have a little job and help me?"

"Well, it depends what it is."

Watt said, "I want you to come and pour tea this afternoon because my hostess just quit."

Thornton said, "Oh, why not? English girls should be able to pour tea." She didn't know it would turn out to be 400 cups of tea because there was a Friesan-Holstein [cattle] convention there. These were the ladies who were being entertained while their husbands were in the meeting. "Little Eleanor" Majewski taught her how to use an urn for tea. "And I poured and I poured and I poured and she handed them out and gave them one cookie apiece. She was a great disciplinarian!"

Thornton did the bus tours with the ladies. She had to learn the history of things fast. One lady who sat on the back of the bus hesitated to exit when the rest did. Thornton thought, "Oh dear. Here comes an embarrassment. I'm going to get a dollar."

The lady said, "I just want you to know that I've lived all over the world. I've seen the Andes. I've seen the Tetons. I've, you know, been in the Alps. But I have never been anywhere like Lake Placid and the Adirondacks. This is a wonderful area. You can rest your eyeballs here." Thornton thought it was a strange description but where the woman had lived, everything had been pointed and craggy.

During a convention in the 1970s the buffet was to be set up outdoors. One of the convention representatives came storming out and said to Thornton, "Look at this table! they're going to be here in 15 minutes and there's nothing on it!"

Thornton thought and said, "Well, I can explain that. We have a lot of chipmunks and squirrels here so we can't put food out too early otherwise they'd get it before the guests." and to herself she said, "Phew! Let a hole open up and bury me!" She went into the kitchen, shared the story with them and said, "Come on, let's get this stuff out before the chipmunks do arrive!"

Just before the 1980 Olympics, Thornton met representatives from 5 different corporations who asked her to do specific things to the cottages like engage the decorator for Theanoguen so it could be used by American Express during the Olympics. She then worked with the attached lodges at the Club and formed Brief Encounters to continue doing so.

Was the work worth it? Malcolm Alford, bellman, said working at the Club was one of his most pleasant experiences. "I felt it was character forming and gave me insight into the world that I could never have obtained in the rather isolated Adirondacks. I was born and raised in Lake Placid, attended St. Lawrence University and graduated from the University of Arizona. I am a retired geologist having returned to Lake Placid some 20 years ago."

Cornelia Bonsignore from the Club library reflected that half the townspeople worked at the Club and most wouldn't have furthered their education if they hadn't earned money at the Club for college. It was an opportunity to mingle with guests that brought rewarding and educational opportunities and many pleasant times.

CHAPTER THE LAST

"Lake Placid Club, Good Evening"

"...If the buildings on both sides (of the new fireproof tower housing the Club switchboard) were entirely burned, the operators could stay at their posts in safety." (Club Notes, April 1918)

Club Notes do not record (nor could it be printed here!) what the switchboard operators said about staying at their posts while fire raged around them! This statement of Melvil Dewey's does underscore the centrality of communication to the Club, dependence upon the switchboard operators, and it acknowledges the number one fear of Adirondack hotels: fire.

Six La France chemical fire engines, pumps and big streams in 1909 were the heart of the fire equipment operated by the Club. The chemical used to extinguish fires was a mixture of sulfuric acid and soda that generated carbon dioxide. There were three fire companies that held weekly drills and monthly exhibits of their firefighting prowess. The Club grounds were divided into six wards and six fire districts with automatic fire alarm boxes. The fire brigade officer was on duty all night at the telephone exchange in Forest Hall. There was a big fire bell, steam fire whistle and telephone connections to all cottages and central points. The Fire Code had 52 pages (expanded to 74 pages in 1914) and an index of 519 entries giving minute directions. As a consequence of this preparation and fear of fire by employees, in June of 1909, "The decision is final to replace smokers by non-smokers, for we cannot afford the extra risk involved in having employees [smoking] about our flammable buildings."

Club Notes reported, "The prompt and efficacious response of Club and village fire departments to a midnight alarm May 6,1930 prevented the 82nd Club fire from fighting its stubborn way to more serious damage of Overlook and completely protected nearby buildings from harm. The speed with which firemen unreeled hose and had eight 2 1/2 inch streams playing to the top of the tall building was reminiscent of the monthly prize fire drills held close to that same spot. Overlook was unoccupied, cleaners had been working there that day but cause of the fire is not known. The Cafeteria on the ground floor where 300 of the Club staff eat in summer was unharmed and bedrooms on the two floors above will be repaired for summer use."

Elsa Bombard, who worked the switchboard from 1946 to 1979, did have a fire call on her shift. A rack held disks of every location at the Club. The disk locating the fire was to be taken out, put in another place connected to the alarm and the alarm pulled. This one time Bombard had to do it, the disk flew out of her hands across the room. She chased it, put it in the right place and pulled the alarm. There were frequent fire drills orchestrated by the Club in cooperation with the fire department and the fire team at the Club. In wooden hotels featuring fireplaces, fire was a very real danger but during Mildred Pelkey Kelly's watch (1950 to 1974) there were no fires.

Operators once dealt with a bomb threat that was phoned in during off season. The State Police were called first and then John Watt, Club manager. A search did not turn up a bomb.

For medical emergencies, Dr. Hart would be called and the operators knew the office hours he kept at the Club six days a week. He was very good at letting the switchboard know when he would be away. At one lunchtime, a long-time bellman had a heart attack. The operator called for help at the same time Club manager John Watt was calling her. She told him she couldn't help him then. Watt called a second time and the operator told him what had happened. He rushed to the bellman and later told the operator she had done the right thing.

Usually things were more routine and calm. There were two operators on each shift and a chief operator. Mildred Kelly worked under chief operator Ethel Murphy for one year and then Kelly became chief operator. Grace Lawrence Chabbott worked on the switchboard for 25 years, 1955 to 1980 and became chief after Kelly. The Club closed after foliage season and re-opened for the winter. The first couple of years Chabbott went on unemployment during that time but then worked year round. The chief operator would handle problems and questions such as "When is tea served?" or provide directions. Two types of calls were received, those from within the Club which were greeted with, "Number, please" and those incoming from overtown which evoked, "Lake Placid Club, may I help you?" Shifts were 7 a.m. to 3 p.m., 3 to 11 p.m., and 11p.m. to 7 a.m. Six to 11 p.m. was a difficult time as guests called one another to cocktails and dinner. In summer that was an additional shift. There were part-time girls who could be called in when needed. Kelly would go back to help in a 6 to 11p.m. shift but generally two operators could handle it. The shifts were not carved in stone and during conventions, shifts were adjusted to provide timely coverage of two on the board and one at the desk. At first Bombard worked 6 to 11 p.m. and then went full time. Bernice Lawrence Lacey, Virginia Gilmore's mother, was a telephone operator at night. A bachelor gentleman also worked the switchboard from 11 p.m. to 7 a.m. It was assumed that the bag he always carried had his lunch in it. However, Kelly would be called to the front desk because guests complained that at night they were getting strange responses from the switchboard.

One night Chabbott suspected he had been drinking so when he relieved her, she waited. She heard him saying, "Answer me, damn you!" but he didn't have the earphones and speaker on. She called Kelly and told her he couldn't stay alone on the switchboard that night. The situation was taken care of.

Operators sat on high revolving stools in front of the old-style Western Electric switchboard, which was a panel about 15 feet long full of round holes. Operators worked cords with plugs that fit the holes and wore earphones with an attached speaker. Calls would be received when the board lit up. The plug would be inserted, the key pushed forward to make the connection and pulled back to ring the receiving phone.

Operators had a large board called a "visible" in back of them. Each morning operators would check at the front desk for new arrivals. Guest cards were filed alphabetically in the visible. When a call was received, the operator would swing around to find where the requested person was. If the guest was not in his room, the operator would call the front desk who then asked the bellman to page the guest. As a general rule, guests were very nice. There were, however, some guests whose names the operators were glad to see on the checkOUT list!

Club operators worked with overtown operators who worked for N. Y. Telephone. Long distance calls would come through the overtown operators who told the Club which guest to charge. There were very few transatlantic calls.

Around 1975 the Club installed a new electronic Hitachi switchboard. The operators panicked and said they would never be able to do this but learning didn't take too long. Their friends from N.Y. Telephone overtown helped teach them how to just push buttons. "It was not so much fun! " Chabbott bemoaned. Then the operators wore headphones and a little wire to pick up the voice.

The kitchen was awfully good to the switchboard operators and would frequently send up coffee and pastry. At dinner time, Jeanette, who was in charge of tray service, would come in and ask, "What would you like tonight, Honey?" and then from time to time she would add, "You don't want the potato salad!"

In the summer the operators had fans to keep them cool and in the winter, they had lots of heat. Winter times were slow but the operators kept busy. Bombard knit many sweaters and made a rug. "In the summer, there was no time to do things like that!"

At first there was no bathroom and the operators would use the hall bathroom but in the early 1960s they got their own bathroom.

Parties were great, especially the children's party at Christmas. In Bombard's day, the employee children got real presents of toys (not a deposit to a bank account) and really looked forward to the Christmas party. Operators would go out to dinner together but except for Christmas, they did not party at the Club with other staff. Operators could hear the Saturday night concerts from the switchboard. There were Christmas parties in the office and presents exchanged. Charlie was in charge of the eggnog punch bowl and one year had just added the rum and went to move the punchbowl in small quarters with lots of people around. They heard a "ping" and the punch bowl burst. There was scrambling to wipe up the mess. The front desk was called to send up housekeeping with mops and pails. The switchboard office enjoyed the aroma of rum for weeks!

Work at the Club was always fun. Most operators had children. Bombard raised three children while working there. One operator worked 6 to 11 p.m. because she had someone then to take care of her children during those hours. While she was on duty, a call came through from her family. She answered and, by mistake, had opened two keys. In response to the house problem, she told both her child and the Club manager, "Take off your pants." There was some sputtering from one of the parties!

There was a summer program for children of members, Parkside Riding Academy, which took children on trail rides. Millie Kelly loved to ride so she went and held up the rear of the line of children on horses. They had to watch Caesar, the horse, more than the children because he liked to try to lie down with a kid on his back!

Kelly was also an Auxiliary Lake Placid police officer. When she was called to police duty, she had to get coverage for the board. Her responsibility was to "baby-sit" women in trouble in the lockup or those waiting to get out. "It was a fun job working with screaming females!" She was also on duty in uniform at functions in the Olympic Arena. The fellows in the Police Department kidded her and called her their token female in the 1970s.

Mildred Kelly was the first woman to graduate from the North Country Community College (NCCC) criminal justice program and while still working the 7 a.m. to 3 p.m. shift at the Club, would leave work, grab a sandwich and go down to SUNY Plattsburg to take classes there from 7 to 9:30 p.m. She earned a Bachelor's degree and began teaching criminal justice and sociology at Clinton Community College in 1974. She was sad to leave the Club because "everyone was always good to us." She received her Master's degree from Goddard College, Vermont in 1979 and in 1987 was honored for her outstanding teaching at the NCCC Elizabethtown facility. She also received honors from the Lake Placid Police Department Auxiliary and was recognized by her students as an outstanding and caring teacher. In 1993, she was given a distinguished Alumnus award by NCCC and the College also gives a Mildred Pelkey Kelly award to an outstanding student in the criminal justice field.

The switchboard office was the gathering place for N.Y. Telephone repairmen Bernie Wheeler and Bob LaHart. LaHart came in to take care of problems but appreciated lunch, too. Security men (George Sheffield was Night Security) who were on duty all day and night talked with the operators. Security could be called for emergencies anywhere in the Club. They would go around inside the Club, patrol outside and sat out by the front desk.

One of the last managers, hired to close the Club, was a miserable person because of what he had to do and how he did it. He called for his secretary. There was no answer. He asked for the front desk. There was no answer. He asked, "Isn't anyone working?"

The operator replied, "I'm working."

He responded, "I mean somebody, not you!"

He was not well liked.

Just before the Olympics in 1980, Bombard and Chabbott worked the board by themselves seven days a week. They brought their own lunch and drinks. They were not being paid for overtime or given time off. Young people would be hired to help but weren't interested in the job and wouldn't come in on time. Bombard and Chabbott had had it! Evelyn Smith, who lived in Keesville 35 or 40 miles away, came in six nights a week to be the night operator. When Bombard and Chabbott had had enough and were quitting, they called Smith, who said, "Good! I'm not coming in either!" They turned off the switchboard, the instrument that held the Club together. They silenced the Club communication system, and walked off the job.

Once at the Annex, they realized they had left something in the office and needed to get it out. They certainly weren't going back.

Club employees, however, always worked together. Someone in housekeeping went to the switchboard and, from the window-sill, retrieved the can of beer.

AFTERWORD

The Lake Placid Club did not die a graceful death. It clung to its restrictions and traditions tenaciously until 1977 when it opened its doors to all the public with the expectation that hoi polloi would come. "The people" did not come. Values and vacation styles had changed while the doors had been closed to so many.

Operating as the The Lake Placid Resort Hotel, the institution made it through the 1980 Winter Olympics with infusions from corporate Olympic sponsors.

The gumption of Club employees continued as Grace Chabbott walked overtown and was hired by the American Broadcasting Company as a switchboard operator during the 1980 Olympics. Elsa Bombard became receptionist and switchboard operator at the Lake Placid Hospital, now Adirondack Medical Center.

The Resort Hotel defaulted on loans, and bankruptcy was declared.

One developer, John R. Swaim, promoted time shares and expansion only to be convicted of fraud and sentenced to federal prison.

Hopes of the locals were high that a Gleneagles Hotel Lake Placid [Guinness Beer Company] would come into being but negotiations were not successful.

Suspicious fires did the damage that the Club fire guard had prevented for 85 years. Fire destroyed Theanoegen in 1991, small Club buildings were torched in 1992, and the main portion of Forest, damaged by fire, was demolished in 1993. An arson fire damaged Larches, (a Club cottage), and the Mt. Whitney Ski Lodge was destroyed by fire in 1995.

The grand and joyful Club was seen by a generation of high school students such as Chris Morris as "the old haunted abandoned building" and a destination for friends who liked to hike through the deserted halls.

The Lussi family bought the Club in 1996.

January 2002 closed more doors for the final time when Agora Theater, the Chapel and Agora Suites were demolished to make the site more appealing for development.

The Club boat house, now beautifully renovated and decorated with plaques from the Annie Godfrey Dewey Memorial Chapel, is a delightful restaurant with outdoor and indoor dining.

The Lake Placid Club Links Course, now irrigated, (Lower 7,006 total yards - par 71), Mountain Course (Upper 6,156 total yards- par 70) and Pristine (Short) 9 holes continues to welcome golfers in proper golf attire. Beautiful mountain scenery contributes to the peaceful setting and "Large boulders are intergal part of course." No caddies are employed.

In due time and in the style of the 21st century, foundations will disturb the shards of French plate glass and new employee memories will grow along the east shore of Mirror Lake in the Village of Lake Placid, Town of North Elba, in upstate New York.

SOURCES

INTERVIEWS

Ackerman, David
Albright, Annette
Albright, Philip
Anonymous Club Employee
Baker, Howard
Beauregard, George
Blair, Linda
Blanchard, Robert
Bombard, Elsa
Bonsignore, Cornelia
Bowhall, Roscoe
Brown, Carol
Bryant, Imogene
Chabbott, Grace
Devlin, Art
Donnellan, Ray
Dorin, Peg
Dunn, Araxie
Forest, Lisa
Gilmore, Virginia
Happel, Dorothy
Hart, Dr. George
Hart, Mrs.
Howe, Agnes
Huttlinger, Anne
Hutweiler, Jan Elliott
Kelly, Mildred
Lansing, John
Lansing, Mickey
Lawrence, Allen,
Lewis, Cal
Lussi, Sergei
Kendrick, Jack
McCasland, Blanche
Mclntrye, Ray
McLean, Debbie
Maxwell, Sidney Leach
Moody, Tom
Peters, Karen
Preston, Leona
Purchase, Harry
Reid, Beverly
Reynolds, Robert
Richards, Fred
Sileo, Jim
Silleck, Frances
Stevens, Marjorie
Strack, Barbara Downes
Sweeney, Bob
Thornton, Audrey
van Hoesin, David
Wallace, Mary
Wareham, Alice
Wilson, Calvin
Wilson, Elizabeth

e-mail

Alford, Malcolm
Baker, Howard
Beck, Cyndi
Gilmore, Virginia
Hatfield, George
Hughes, Liz
Lucas, Ian
McKeen, Jim
McMorris, Paul
Mussari, Marilyn
Nientimp, Tom
Rawdon, Andy

LETTERS

Androski, Hazel "Skippy"
Durkee, Norma Welter
MacKenzie, Mary
Peters, Karen Marshall

BOOKS

Ackerman, David H, Lake Placid Club, an Illustrated History 1895 -1980, Lake Placid
Education Foundation, 1998
Carroll, George, Lake Placid, Thomas F. Barton, Publisher, Glens Falls, N.Y. 1968
Club Notes, 1905-1935
Lake Placid Club Handbook 1901
MacKenzie, Mary, Lake Placid and North Elba, A History, The Bookstore Plus, Lake Placid, N.Y. 2002

PHOTOS

Barry Collection in the Lake Placid Center for the Arts
Campbell Collection
Hatfield, George
Peters, Karen Marshall
Sileo, Jim
Lake Placid Club Archives

DOCUMENTS

Dewey, Annie, An Address on Euthenics and Its Founder, First National Conference on Race Betterment, Battle Creek, Michigan, January 1914

Dewey, Godfrey, Sixty Years of Lake Placid Club

Dewey, Godfrey & Margaret, Iroquois Indian Council, 1972

Files of Mary MacKenzie, Retired Lake Placid & North Elba Historian

Fish, Howard, The Last Dance, a Funeral March for the 93 Year Old Lake Placid Club; Adirondack Life, March/April 1987

Harrison, Joseph L, Melvil Dewey, An Appreciation, 1932

Lake Placid Club Archives, Lake Placid Public Library, Lake Placid, N.Y.

Lake Placid Club Chambermaids Directions, April 1918 & June 1929

Lake Placid Club Directions for Bel servis, February 1918

Lake Placid Club To Employees of Uniformed Service

New York State Census, 1905, 1915, 1925

Manchester, Lee, LP Golf havens and heavens, Lake Placid News, June 22, 2001

Felt, Paul, ed. The Placid Dish, 1938

The Rise and Fall of the Lake Placid Club, essays by Buxton, Campbell, Crowley, Hart, Manchester, Morris, Rauch; Adirondack Daily Enterprise, January 2002

United States Census 1910, 1920